LINCOLN CHRISTIAN COLLEGE AND SEMINARY

W9-BVE-854

A Second Resurrection

A Second Resurrection

Leading Your Congregation
to
New Life

BILL EASUM

ABINGDON PRESS
NASHVILLE

A SECOND RESURRECTION
LEADING YOUR CONGREGATION TO NEW LIFE

Copyright © 2007 by Abingdon Press

All rights reserved.
No part of this work may be reproduced or transmitted in any form or by any means, electronic or mechanical, including photocopying and recording, or by any information storage or retrieval system, except as may be expressly permitted by the 1976 Copyright Act or in writing from the publisher. Requests for permission should be addressed to Abingdon Press, P.O. Box 801, 201 Eighth Avenue South, Nashville, TN 37202-0801 or permissions@abingdonpress.com.

This book is printed on acid-free paper.

Library of Congress Cataloging-in-Publication Data

Easum, William M., 1939-
   A second resurrection : leading your congregation to new life / Bill Easum.
      p. cm.
   Includes bibliographical references and index.
   ISBN 978-0-687-64653-1 (binding: pbk. : alk. paper)
1. Church renewal.   I. Title.

   BV600.3.E275 2007
   253—dc22

                                                              2007012912

All scripture quotations unless noted otherwise are taken from the HOLY BIBLE, NEW INTERNATIONAL VERSION®. NIV®. Copyright © 1973, 1978, 1984 by International Bible Society. Used by permission of Zondervan Publishing House. All rights reserved.

07 08 09 10 11 12 13 14 15 16—10 9 8 7 6 5 4 3 2 1
MANUFACTURED IN THE UNITED STATES OF AMERICA

CONTENTS

1/83

116790

PREFACE

I am not afraid that the people called Methodists [insert the name of your tribe] should ever cease to exist either in Europe or America. But I am afraid lest they should only exist as a dead sect, having the form of religion without the power. And this undoubtedly will be the case unless they hold fast both the doctrine, spirit, and discipline with which they first set out. John Wesley

For many congregational and denominational leaders, the goal for churches experiencing declining worship attendance is to turn those congregations around. The "turnaround church" is one that has stagnated or is in decline. The old trends are reversed, new members are added, and everyone rejoices in this story of a congregation restored to health and vitality.

But what if the metaphors of decline, stagnation, and loss of health just aren't getting to the problem? What if the situation is much worse than what those ways of describing it imply? What if the congregation is spiritually dead?

The only solution is resurrection. Churches that have lost their sense of mission, that exist only to provide fellowship for the "members of the club," that expect their leaders to focus solely on ministering to the members' personal spiritual needs—these churches have died to the purpose of the New Testament church, to make disciples of Jesus Christ. They cannot be turned around; they must come to life again. The key to that resurrection is leaders who are not afraid to diagnose the problem for what it really is, and who realize that resurrection is what being a Christian is about.

My goal is to guide the leaders of these churches through the painful yet ultimately life-giving work of leading a church to new life in the Spirit.

If you want to find new life for your church, read on. . . .

INTRODUCTION

Whatever wisdom I can share with you in this book comes from two sources:

- The church I turned around in 1969 and was privileged to pastor for twenty-four years;

- The consultations I've had with over 600 churches during my almost twenty years as a consultant.

My experience has taught me the resurrection of a church happens in three stages. It begins with a new pastor. Either the pastor experiences a personal resurrection or the church actually gets a new pastor. Next is the resurrection of the leaders of the church either by transformation or replacement. Finally, the church itself is resurrected and turned around through some tactical change. I've never seen a turnaround that does not follow this pattern.

Most of my earlier books addressed mainly the final stage of turnaround without addressing the issue of spiritual bankruptcy and the need for resurrection. I always knew that revitalization wasn't the answer, but I was not as clear on the issue of spiritual bankruptcy and resurrection as I am today.

The spiritual condition of established Protestantism has gotten much worse over the last few years. So my most recent books have focused more on the spiritual dimension of turnaround. *Put on Your Own Oxygen Mask First* addressed the first stage of resurrection in detail—the spiritual life of the pastor. *Unfreezing Moves* began the renewal of the church with the spiritual depth of the leadership. This book goes even further and focuses on resurrection rather than turnaround. Most established churches are spiritually bankrupt. Therefore, the most basic need of the vast majority of established churches is resurrection.

Who This Book Is For

This book is not meant to be read by or with just anyone. It is meant to be read by a pastor and group of laypeople who long for their church to turn around from its decline.

Because of its frankness I suggest that a pastor read it first, then gather a group from the church (the remnant) who long for the turnaround, and read and discuss the book with them. Then begin the long journey of turnaround of the church.

Thank You

Over these fifty-odd years of ministry, I've been privileged to work with many wonderful Christians who have taught me much. To those laypeople in the early years of my pastorate at Colonial Hills United Methodist Church and to the pastors and laypeople of the many turnaround consultations, I say, "Thank you for what you have taught me and God bless you for your courage to believe all things are possible with Christ."

I also want to thank the following members of EBA Community who gave of their time to read the original draft and offer suggestions: Mike Thompson, John Atkinson, Sue Allen, Stephen Portner, Steve Cordle, Ingrid Kutsch, Jan Blankenship, John Guilfoyle, Guido Neil Climer, Edward Boyce, Eddie Hammett, Michael Deutsch, Steve Ross, Doyll Andrews, Dale Turner, John Randalls, Mike Hicks, and Jim Zimmerman. Their participation made this a better book.

Bill Easum
Port Aransas, TX
2006

CHAPTER ONE

When It's Not a Matter of Sickness

Let those who have ears to hear, hear.

Ridiculous!" he screamed as I explained to him the plan for this book. "You can't compare turning around an established church with the resurrection of Jesus Christ! That's sacrilege!" he shouted as he stomped out of the room.

Obviously this person has never experienced the pain of trying to turn around an established church. Nothing can be more difficult. I hear this difficulty echoed in the testimony of every turnaround pastor with whom I talk or consult (and I've consulted on-site with hundreds of pastors who wanted to turn around their churches). Sure, turnaround can't literally be compared to Jesus' resurrection. But metaphorically it most definitely can. If you've tried to turn a church around, you know what I mean. But let me explain more fully.

Revitalization Is Not the Answer

For much of the past three decades, denominational officials have been promoting seminars and programs aimed at revitalizing the church. I know because I have been the speaker or consultant to many of these groups. For many of these leaders, their goal was to breathe new life into churches experiencing declining memberships and lack of commitment. Yet after years of trying to revitalize these churches, the vast majority of them are still declining. What gives?

Is it possible we have underestimated the seriousness of Western Protestantism's situation? What if the metaphors of reformation, renewal, and revitalization don't get to the heart of the problem? What if the situation is much worse than those words describe? *What if the vast majority of congregations in the West are spiritually dead and God no longer considers them to be churches? What if God has one foot out the door of most of Western Protestantism? What if the vast majority of our churches are like the church of Laodicea in the Book of Revelations? What if God is about to spit us out of his mouth?*[1]

Reformation, renewal, and revitalization assume some pre-existing foundation of faith from which to raise up a new church. But what if that assumption isn't correct? What if the assumption is part of our problem? What if being a member of a church for forty years doesn't automatically guarantee any spiritual depth? What if holding every office in the church doesn't automatically mean someone is a disciple of Jesus Christ? Do we dare look deep enough into our souls to find answers to these questions?

Based on the conversations and actions of the thousands of Protestant leaders with whom I worked over the years, I have concluded that most of them are spiritually dead and their institutions have ceased being the church. They have the form but not the substance of what it means to be the church.

Perhaps you're wondering how I define a "spiritually dead church." What you must keep in mind is that churches are nothing more than people who have come together. So when I refer to "church" I am not referring to the institution, but to the people who make up the church. Christianity is a movement of people who have come together in a group for a purpose. So I'm not talking about the resurrection of an institution. I'm talking about the resurrection of the people who make up the institution. They are the ones who are spiritually dead.

I have never seen a church where every member is spiritually dead. A remnant seems to always exist. But overall, the actions of the church are void of any spirituality. Every church has those who remain spiritually focused, enthused, and on fire no matter how complacent those around them may grow. The key is to tap into those folks and grow their number. More on this later.

So let me define what I mean by spiritually dead churches. Here are some clues. Spiritually dead churches

- Have lost their sense of mission to those who have not heard about Jesus Christ and do not pant after the Great Commission;

- Exist primarily to provide fellowship for the "members of the club";

- Expect their pastors to focus primarily on ministering to the members' personal spiritual needs;

- Design ministry to meet the needs of their members;

- Have no idea about the needs of the "stranger outside the gates";

- Are focused more on the past than the future;

- Often experience major forms of conflict;

- And watch the bottom line of the financial statement more than the number of confessions of faith.

> **Trying to decide if your church is spiritually dead? Let me give you a hint: if your church spends most of its energy on itself and its members, it's spiritually dead.**

Such churches are living corpses. They are physically alive; some may even be growing; but they are spiritually dead to the mission of the New Testament church—to make disciples of Jesus Christ. They've turned inward and exist solely for themselves. They look for ways to serve themselves, and the kingdom be damned. They're like baby birds sitting in the nest with their mouths open waiting for momma bird (pastor) to feed them with no concept that Jesus intends them to feed others. Oh, they might collect money to send away to some distant mission field, but they're all thumbs when it comes to sharing the good news with their neighbor or community. What growth they might experience is not of their doing—it just happens because of the population growth around them.

The Hidden Truth

Underneath all of the tactics and programs in a consultant's bags of tricks, lies something rarely talked about—the abundance of selfish leaders and the lack of spiritually obedient leaders, both lay and clergy. (I hate using those terms.) Most churches have copped out to democratic rule and corporate behaviors instead of following the biblical principles of discernment and prayer. Our churches nominate and elect people to committees and boards without the slightest idea of the depth of their private spiritual life. We allow people to vote on the future of the church who haven't disciplined their lives, much less prayed about the issue. We have so many checks and balances we make it impossible for the Holy Spirit to move among us. And we wonder why we're in the mess we're in.

The following email is indicative of dozens of emails I receive each year.

Subject:	Re: thanks
Date:	7/11/2006 10:33:50 A.M. Central Standard Time
From:	anyone@ hotmail.com
To:	easum@aol.com

When It's Not a Matter of Sickness

Dear Bill and Tom,

Thank you for the books you have written and the seminars you have led. They helped shape my ministry for the past several years. However, if I were two years older or much younger today I would probably leave the ministry and find something else to do.

I tried to lead my last church to change and was reappointed to the most tension-filled, control-oriented church I have ever served. I don't mind the tension or facing the controllers. We have been successful in this regard. At both my last church and this church, eventually in the midst of change, the most healthy, respected, and potentially effective leaders quit to go to large churches with a full menu of programs.

It is not my preaching that causes them to leave nor my basic personality. They usually leave to follow their wives or children to a church that currently offers them what they need/want. I am really frustrated this morning, as the most respected and strongest layperson let others know what I already knew, that he was leaving to follow his wife to a successful church in a neighboring town.

I really have doubts that any churched people want to have a compelling vision; it might cost too much for them to fulfill it. I will probably stay here a little longer and watch a few more people who could have been key players leave, then I will go to another church and play "Pastor Fetch" until I retire. Yuck!

I am not upset with you or the laypeople who leave, or the system for that matter. The problem is within me and my lack of wisdom, leadership gifts, and ability to inspire people. What I hope to see happen is simply elusive and seemingly unattainable for me—to help a congregation become a vital, alive Body of Christ impacting the community in positive ways.

Thanks for sharing your wisdom.

I began addressing the spiritual condition of churches in my book *Unfreezing Moves* where I suggested the starting point for unfreezing a stuck organizational system is the development of a solid community of faith that included spiritual leaders, the absence of major conflict, trust, and a desire to connect with the unchurched world.

I suggested that true spiritual maturity was approached when people turned their attention to those outside the church and sought ways to spread the good news rather than exercise their entitlements as members. Unfortunately, too many pastors assume their church has spiritual leaders and skip right over this starting point. It has become apparent to me that most church leaders do not understand that the decline of their church is due to the lack of spiritual depth on the part of their leadership.

So, now, I want to go deeper on the spiritual issue. It's not just that our churches are stuck; they are spiritually bankrupt!

I know. These churches are filled mostly with good Christian people, but there's no discernable spiritual power, just good Christian people—and we all know what Jesus said about being good.[2]

So it's obvious. Isn't it? *The only solution for spiritually dead congregations is resurrection.* You can't revitalize something that is dead. *They must be brought to life again!* And that is resurrection.

Revitalization is a waste of time. You can't breathe life into a corpse. Only God can do that, and that is resurrection.

But if resurrection happens our behavior changes:

- The church turns outward in its focus.

- Jesus, not the institution, will become the object of our affection.

- The Great Commission will become our mandate, and we will measure everything we do by how many new converts we make rather than whether we have a black bottom line.

- Membership in the Kingdom will replace membership in the church.

- Pastors will cease being chaplains of pastoral care and will become modern-day apostles of Jesus Christ.

- And those who try to control the church with an iron fist or intimidate the church at every turn of the road will be shown the door.

But what about the immigrant church? Many of today's denominations started out as immigrant churches. Immigrant churches were never about reaching out and making disciples. They were started to meet the religious needs of a particular community of people. These people were defined by a particular culture and language. Initially worship was in the native language and reflected the style and music of the "homeland." The assumption was, "Of course people will come here." And they did, because the church was their only connection to their native land. Even the transition in worship from the native language to English was prompted by internal considerations—the young people no longer spoke the original language.

In many of these churches the major outreach was to help new immigrants as they adapted to the dominant culture. Those who had been in the U.S. longer would help the new folks learn how to survive in an alien cultural context. The pastor's time was always to be spent in ministry with the members of the congregation and their families. There was no expectation that the pastor would be engaged in reaching out to disciple new folks. Growth was accidental or biological.

It's my contention that these were dead churches from the beginning. Their intentions were good, but their execution was flawed. They were faithful to the Great Commandment but not the Great Commission. Both are required to be a spiritually faithful church.

Reformation Is Not the Answer Either

Much has been written lately about our being in the midst of a second reformation. Some believe the First Reformation was about freeing the church from the institution and the Second Reformation is about freeing God's people from the church.

Not so. The First Reformation did not free the church from the institution. Instead, slavery to our institutions is *the* primary sin of our time. Most of our people love their buildings more than their God, to the point of making an eleventh commandment necessary: "Thou shalt not love thy buildings more than thy God." Most of our churches are too spiritually dead to be reformed. Reformation isn't the answer.

Denial Is Futile

My grandfather on my mother's side died from a curable disease. He had a skin cancer on his ear lobe, and he refused to get it cut out. Instead, he tried to cure it with a home remedy. It didn't work. The cancer grew into his ear and ultimately into his brain, and he died. His skin cancer was curable; he didn't need to die, but he did.

Most established Protestant leaders and churches are like my grandfather. Like the ostrich, they have buried their heads in the sand, denying the reality any idiot can recognize—something is terribly wrong with our churches. Like my grandfather, if we continue to deny the problem and try to tinker with it ourselves (revitalization) we will needlessly go the way of my grandfather.

> **I know this is tough language and some readers may be offended. But don't stop reading. The more you are offended the more likely you are to need what follows.**

My prayer is that you will respond like the person did in the following email, sent after reading a draft of this chapter.

Subject:	pondering leadership
Date:	4/14/2006 10:07:08 P.M. Central StandardTime
From:	Anyone@USA.com
To:	trnldr@lists.easumbandy.com

"This is a painful read for one who for several years felt she would be able to 'revitalize' a broken church, then realized that if it were ever to live God would have to resurrect it."

The primary reason society is shunning the institutional church is because for the most part it is spiritually dead. Spiritually alive churches, no matter what their form or where they are planted, always grow. That is the nature of the beast. That is the kind of church God honors. That is what the church was put on earth to do—spread the good news. When a church faithfully does that, it grows. Period.

If your church isn't growing, don't take offense. Instead ask yourself why? Does it spend the vast majority of its time figuring out and executing ways to spread the good news? Does it understand that it exists for those who are not yet part of it? Does it pray daily for the spiritual and social redemption of the community? If not, it's spiritually dead, no matter how well it takes care of its members. Unless, of course, it is really a hospice or hospital and not a church!

Priests Don't Handle Dead People

The Old Testament is full of rules regarding what a priest can and can't do. The goal of these rules was to keep God's people holy and clean. Everything was divided up by five categories— Very Holy, Holy, Clean, Unclean, Very Unclean. In order to remain holy, and lead the people, the priest had to avoid all contact with people who were unclean and very unclean. Among the very unclean were people who had major impurities or were dead. If a priest was to touch a dead person that priest became unclean and thus unholy and unfit to lead the people.

Do you see where I'm going with this? Pastors who spend most of their time with spiritually dead people become unfit to lead.

The one thing you can't do is remain the pastor of a spiritually dead church. If you do it will drain you of your spirituality. It's my opinion that that's what has happened to the majority of clergy in established denominations. They have handled dead people so long they have become spiritually dead and are content with being funeral directors.

If you want to be one of God's leaders, then you have only two choices—resurrect the church or get out of Dodge.

So what do you do with spiritually dead people who refuse resurrection? You ignore them. Whatever it takes, you don't let them set the agenda for you or the church.

The Basic Law of Congregational Life

In my first book, years ago, I shared what I considered to be the basic law of congregational life: *"Churches grow when they intentionally reach out to people instead of concentrating on their institutional needs; churches die when they concentrate on their own needs."*[3]

The basic law of congregational life still holds today because it is as biblical as one gets. Spiritually dead churches selfishly care for themselves; spiritually alive churches reach out to those who are not yet part of them. It's that simple.

What This Book Is About

This is a no-nonsense book about the resurrection of spiritually dead churches. Our journey will focus on the spiritual dimension of turnaround without ignoring the basic tactical issues that we know have the potential to grow spiritually alive churches. However, my comments on the tactical issues will be confined to chapter 2. For now I want to focus your attention on the spiritual life of the congregation. I have learned from experience that church leaders do not understand the crucial importance of the spiritual dimension and want to go directly to the tactical issues. Such procedure seldom works. Too many leaders look for the next magical program that will bring life to their churches. Programs may work for a while, but soon they cease being productive because they seldom produce spiritual people. The people may know more about the Scriptures or even about Jesus, but their behavior has not been molded and modified to the point that they care more about the people in the surrounding community than they care about themselves. Inward-focused churches are spiritually dead no matter how busy they are![4]

Who Should Read This Book

More than any of my previous books, this one should be read by every leader in your church. The more people who digest and internalize the contents, the more likely your church will experience a turnaround. I suggest you read this book in the company of a small group of leaders who you feel are the most mature Christians in the church. (I will say more about this group later.) Then move as a group into the next phase and read together my book *Unfreezing Moves*.[5]

The Research

This book is based on my personal experiences in being God's agent in the resurrection of a church I pastored for twenty-four years, as well as actual research of churches I've had a part in turning around over the years through my work as a consultant. The churches come in all sizes, shapes, and tribes. The only thing they have in common is that they were dying when I came into contact with them. Now they are growing.

Denial or Resistance Will Be Normal

The following email came to me through one of our coaching forums.[6]

Subject:	Pondering leadership
Date:	4/13/2006 10:55:52 A.M. Central Daylight Time
From:	Anyone@world.com
To:	advancedleadership@lists.easumbandy.com

"I have been working this point with the congregation I serve and am met with offense. Is there a way to introduce and invite spiritual growth, and beginning again, without alienating those we seek to serve and train? Even claiming the resurrection of Easter didn't help folks feel the need, and all the while, the church continues to die. I suppose this goes back to a matter of maturity. Many have not committed to lifelong learning, growing in grace, or going on to perfection. Ticket's already been punched!"

My response:

"Yep, and until they are able to realize it is a spiritual thing there isn't much hope. This is where we see the spiritual bankruptcy of the church—leaders who do not understand that their growing relationship to Christ is all that matters to any turnaround. It's not programs or gimmicks but spiritual maturity."

Reflection Time

- **How would you describe your relationship with Jesus Christ?**
- **Is Jesus Christ the hope of the world? If not, why?**
- **Do your leaders have a clear sense of purpose?**
- **Does your church exist primarily for those not yet part of it?**
- **Is your church more focused on those outside the church than in it? If not, why?**
- **Does your leadership understand how the communities around the church think, feel, and live?**

I trust you are beginning to see the picture.

Notes

1. "To the angel of the church in Laodicea write: 'These are the words of the Amen, the faithful and true witness, the ruler of God's creation. I know your deeds, that you are neither cold nor hot. I wish you were either one or the other! So, because you are lukewarm—neither hot nor cold—I am about to spit you out of my mouth.'" (Revelation 3:14-16)

2. "Why do you call me good?" Jesus answered. "No one is good—except God alone." (Mark 10:18)

3. William Easum, *The Church Growth Handbook* (Abingdon Press, 1990), p. 16.

4. Case in point: The United Methodist Church has a wonderful program called Disciple Bible. The first edition of Disciple Bible was intended to bring the students to the point of discovering their spiritual gifts and putting them to use in the church. But someone got the bright idea of writing Disciple Bible II, then III, then IV, then. . . . Each course takes almost forty weeks. So a person could spend four years studying and never leave the classroom to become a useful servant of God's kingdom. Sure, people are learning more about their faith, but faith without works is dead.

5. Bill Easum, *Unfreezing Moves* (Abingdon Press, 2001).

6. To subscribe to one of our forums go to the following Web site: www.easum bandy.com/store/registrations/join_the_eba_community

CHAPTER TWO

Are We Spiritually Dead?

Okay, it's decision time. If you've gotten this far, you're to be congratulated. You've demonstrated a desire to do the very best for your church.

However, the odds are the very people who need to take this book to heart are the very ones who will deny they're spiritually dead. If you've ever received an email from me you know that at the bottom of it is this sentence:*"The unmotivated are impervious to the obvious."*

Some will think you can measure the spiritual vitality of a congregation by how faithfully people attend meetings, or how many chickens were delivered to how many funeral wakes, or how much was raised at the garage sale or quilting party, or. . . . These are natural responses for spiritually dead people. They are blind to the truth and have difficulty grasping spiritual truths. That is, until their sight is restored. And that is resurrection!

Talking about Resurrection Isn't Easy

I shared the original draft of this book with several people before publication. Here are two of the many responses I received back.

Subject:	Re: Pondering Leadership
Date:	6/13/2006 11:43:52 A.M. Central Daylight Time
From:	Anyone@world.com
To:	advancedleadership@lists.easumbandy.com

"Your new book resonates with what I have been thinking about for the last seven months. I've been trying to figure out why, no matter how I explain the turnaround process to my leadership, no matter how many ways I try to express the process and the end results differently, my leadership folks never seem to get the point. They respond to almost anything that I share with them about transformation and turnaround with, 'Yes, but . . .' and I keep saying, 'No buts about it.' About three weeks ago I finally realized I could no longer assume that my leadership folks are mature Christians. I realized that I could know everything possible about systems theory, congregational transformation, turnaround strategies, and the like, but until my folks mature in the faith, UNTIL THEY SEE ME REALLY MATURING IN MY FAITH, I'm wasting my time, for the most part, doing anything else. Your new book confirms what I've been thinking. Now it's time to concentrate on raising up mature spiritual leaders. I guess my first hurdle will be convincing them that attending 'church' for forty years does not guarantee nor indicate that someone is a mature Christian."

Here is another email proving the same point.

Subject:	Pondering Leadership
Date:	6/22/2006 9:43:52 A.M. Central Daylight Time
From:	Anyone@world.com
To:	advancedleadership@lists.easumbandy.com

"Dealing with people who equate years of attending church with spiritual maturity, as someone else said in another post, is one of the most frustrating things I have run into. It is like trying to explain air and atmosphere to fish. It is an alternate reality. They have no mental framework to hang it on. Whatever you say will be misinterpreted or not grasped at all. And they will often shoot the messenger. But that just brings us back to the point of your book. Resurrection. For with resurrection comes new sight. Perhaps you could say that the resurrection of a church is made up of the sum of many, many individual resurrections."

Getting people to buy into the fact that they are spiritually dead isn't going to be easy. Many will simply deny it and turn a deaf ear and start plotting your departure. But those with "ears to hear" will see the wisdom in what you are saying. They have felt it in their gut for some time. They just needed someone to bring it to the forefront.

> **I strongly suggest you gather a group of people who you feel are your most devoted Christians and read through this book with them. Spend some time discussing your feelings and what you think needs to happen throughout the congregation.**

So if you're trying to help yourself or your church decide whether or not you and it are spiritually alive or dead. remember: Jesus has given us only two commandments—love one another and make disciples of all the world (I'm referring here to the Great Commandment and the Great Commission). Congregations can love one another and not focus on making disciples, but congregations can't make disciples without first loving one another. Both have to be at the heart of a congregation for it to be spiritually alive no matter how well-intentioned it might be. If your church spends most of its energy on its own preservation and the care and feeding of its own members, it is spiritually dead.

A Litmus Test

The following test will help you figure out whether or not your church is spiritually dead. Answer the questions as honestly as you can or it will not have any value. I suggest only the leaders of the church take the test. You will find how to score it at the end of this chapter (don't peek).

Section 1

Answer the following questions on a scale of 1 to 10 with 1 being Absolute Agreement and 10 being Absolute Disagreement.

When faced with a decision our leaders always ask, "If we do this, will it introduce more people to Jesus Christ?" _____

Our leadership always prays for God's guidance instead of putting the issue up for a vote. _____

Our people spend more time working in the community on behalf of the Kingdom than going to church meetings. _____

Our leaders care more for the fulfillment of the Great Commission than they do for the survival or health of their local church. _____

Our leaders get more satisfaction over the baptism of one person than they do over a balanced budget. _____

Our church leaders recognize and stop conflict before it gets out of hand. _____

Our church spends as much time, energy, and money reaching out into the community as it does on the membership. _____

Individually, our leaders outwardly reflect a healthy, Jesus-centered interior life. _____

Our leaders can articulate what it is about their relationship with Jesus that their neighbor can't live without knowing. _____

Our leaders are more interested in mentoring and equipping people who want to grow than listening to people who complain. _____

Most of the training in our church is designed to help our people understand and connect with the unchurched. _____

Our people spend a lot of time intentionally praying for spiritual growth and acting on what they hear in prayer. _____

When our people are asked about their church, they answer in a way that shares what God is calling them to do rather than "this is what our church does." _____

Visitors tell us regularly that they have never experienced such hospitality in church before. _____

Prayer is a major part of everything that we do. _____

Our people leave worship inspired to the point that they feel compelled to bring someone with them next week. _____

Even though something may offend our leaders' aesthetic (musical or artistic) taste, they will support it if it will introduce people to Jesus Christ. _____

We have a strong accountability system for our leaders. _____

We never have a blowup in our board meetings. _____

Section 1 Subtotal: _____

Section 2

If a group wanted to plant a church just down the street from our church, we would:

Be upset: Enter 5
Welcome it and not oppose it: Enter 0
Welcome it and ask how we could help: Enter -5

Section 3

If the majority opinion in your congregation reflects two or more of the following statements, add 15 points to your score. If not, add 0 points.

"If we do this we won't know everyone anymore."
"Don't you think we have enough people now?"
"Shouldn't we take better care of who we've got before we go after any more people?"
"I think it is the duty of the pastor to visit everyone in the hospital."
"The pastor is not as visible and convenient as he or she used to be."
"Why doesn't the pastor love us as much as she or he loves people outside the church?"
"Why should we be trained to do ministry? Isn't that why we pay the pastor?"
"I'm not going to be here in twenty years, so why should I want to do anything?"
"We should try to reach out more to our inactive members before going after new people."

Total (add the three cells in gray): _____

Go to the end of this chapter to find out how to score your results.

Don't Continue to Deny the Truth

Let me tell you a story you won't believe. About the second year of my consulting ministry, I worked with a very small dying church of around seventy-five in worship. Only two people were under the age of fifty. The church said it wanted to grow. So I had them do what every dying church usually has to do, we started a new worship service designed to reach the people in the surrounding area. It took them a while to find the musicians and the worship leader, but they did. They had enough money in the bank to do so. (Most dying churches have enough money in the bank to turn themselves around, but they're saving it for a rainy day even though the ark came around three times last month.)

Eighteen months after they started the new service it was larger than the original service. It had 140 people on an average Sunday, and the original service had around forty. They had more than doubled their attendance and assured their viability for some time.

Guess what they did? They cancelled the new service because the members who stayed in the original service were upset at what had happened. Two years later the church could no longer afford a pastor, and it merged with another church. This church was spiritually dead.

Accepting the truth isn't easy.

Reflection Time

Don't take this journey alone. Make a list of the people you would like to invite into a small group to read and discuss this book.

How to Grade the Litmus Test

If your score is 60 and under you are a spiritually healthy congregation.

If your score is between 60-70 you are not spiritually dead but on the way.

If your score is over 70 you are spiritually dead.

However, the lower you score the more spiritually alive your congregation is. So, don't be unconcerned if your scores are slightly over 60.

CHAPTER THREE

How Churches Die Spiritually

I don't believe any church leaders intentionally set out to cause their church to spiritually die. Most church leaders in established churches I've worked with believe their actions are meant to keep their churches alive. However, their actions and decisions do just the opposite. But God wants far more from the church. God doesn't care if our churches survive. God wants our churches to be part of the movement designed to bring the whole creation into submission to God. Anything short of that is failure.

So how did most established Protestant churches become spiritually dead? I've thought a lot about this over the years. Let me share a brief overview of how I think established, Western Protestantism got to where it is today.

Action—A church is planted and passionately looks for new members. Everything it does is designed to reach new people. Soon it begins to grow. Baptisms are celebrated. Excitement is everywhere. The future is bright. Leaders aren't afraid to take risks. The pastor functions like a spiritual entrepreneur, making many of the day-to-day decisions without the interference of a board or constitution, so things are accomplished in rapid succession. The leaders don't mind if the pastor spends more time in the community than in the office.

Comfort—The church reaches a point where it has enough people to have all the money it needs—usually between 75 and 125 people in worship. It establishes its constitution and bylaws and organizational structure, most of which are concerned with the internal affairs of the congregation rather than the original mission of reaching new people. If the pastor doesn't embed the Great Commission into the DNA of the congregation and personally be a role model for outreach, leaders begin to rely more on the institutional structure, decision-making slows down, and the mission is watered down by congregational consensus. The leaders begin to question the need for more people, and growth begins to plateau. The leaders begin to say: *"If we do this we won't know everyone anymore"*; and *"Don't you think we have enough people now?"* A spiritually alive pastor will respond with something like, "Aren't the real questions, *'Does everyone in town know God?'* and *'Can a church ever have enough people if it is pursuing the Great Commission?'*" However, without such a response from the pastor the church turns inward, and the church begins to die spiritually. If the Great Commission isn't embedded in the leadership, the arrival of a new pastor spells trouble because odds are the new pastor will follow the institutional guidelines and direction of the church leadership rather than the mandate of the gospel. (Don't get mad; that is what I see happening most often.)

Complacency—The church no longer feels an urgent need to reach more people since it has enough money to pay the bills. At this point the church makes a sudden, deadly shift and begins to expect the pastor to be there for *them* rather than to reach new people. They want the pastor in the office more than in the community. The leaders begin to say *"Shouldn't we take better care of who we've got before we go after any more people?"* *"I think it is the duty of the pastor to visit everyone in the hospital."* *"The pastor isn't as visible and convenient as he/she used to be."* *"Why should we be trained to do ministry? Isn't that why we pay the pastor?"* If the pastor gives in, the pastor is now turned into a chaplain rather than an equipper, and the decline begins. The longer the church goes from this point without turnaround, the harder the turnaround becomes until the final stages of life.

Status quo—The church becomes content with the way things are and establishes patterns of behavior designed to keep everything just as it is. The statement *"We've never done that before, and we aren't going to do so now"* becomes the church's mission in life. The leaders like things just as they are and will do almost anything to keep the status quo. A subtle shift begins to happen: the leaders begin to talk more about the needs of their church than about their need of a relationship with Jesus. The entitlements of membership are now celebrated. Their commitment to the institution takes the place of their obedience to God through Jesus Christ. The mandate of the Great Commission is replaced with the mandate to preserve the institution at all costs. The church begins to resemble a club.

Fear of change—The church is so content with the status quo that it fears any kind of change because change would upset the balance of power and cause loss of control. So it clamps down even harder on anything that might upset the status quo or cost any money. It passes rules or policies to prevent bad things from happening. The leaders say to the pastor, *"We should try to reach out more to our inactives before going after new people."* The last thing the leaders want is new blood since it might challenge the status quo. After all, "we're family now." At this point turnaround becomes a battleground seldom won.

Angst over the future—The church begins to realize that it is not as healthy as it once was due to a shortage of money and members. It longs for the good old days when the church was vibrant and healthy (i.e., when they were able to pay the bills). If the church has any money in the bank, it begins to rely on the money as its savior. Line item budgets are read more closely than the Scripture, and guess what happens to people's relationships with Jesus? He is replaced by the culture of fear. At this point God leaves the room and the church is on its own!

Entrenched fearful state—The church hunkers down and guards what little people and money it has instead of addressing the issues. Survival becomes the mission in life, and change becomes the primary enemy. In a world of incremental change such a stance isn't good but it isn't deadly. But in a world of exponential change like the one we live in today, such a stance is deadly. The more the church hunkers down, the faster it declines.

Void of positive leadership—Because of the culture of fear and the loss of any spiritual vitality, the few remaining spiritual leaders, who had held out some hope for the church, leave because they want to be where God is doing something. Without leaders to lead them, the remaining leaders leave the church and the controllers fill the vacuum. Although it's seldom vocalized, the remaining leaders say, *"I'm not going to be here in twenty years, so why should I want to do anything?"* At this point the church is spiritually dead. Only a small, aging remnant remains, and they are seldom in power.

Spiral downward—The church goes into a freefall in all areas of life and ministry and focuses even more on its selfish need to survive. Spiritual death does not happen overnight, nor is it the fault of any one group of people. It takes time for churches to wind up spiritually dead. But take heart: this is the stage that is the most open to resurrection.

Spiritual death does not have to happen. In order for this picture to be reversed, the following usually happens.

Action—Someone (usually the pastor) begins to cast a vision of a different future and gathers together a group of like-minded members to be the leaders of the future. These people may or may not presently be in leadership. Please note: this action is never the result of a committee or board; it will always be one person who decides to become a change agent.

Discomfort—The new vision disrupts the comfort level of the church leaders—a positive step because people are open to change in direct proportion to their level of discontent. The more discontent, the more open to change people are. Rather than trying to smooth over the waters, the leader fans the discontentment of the gathered leaders in whom the Spirit is growing. This is a critical point in the turnaround. If the change agent blinks here, it's all over. The old guard gains strength, and those who hope for change lose their last ounce of courage.

It's not unusual in this stage for the pastor to create one or two quick victories. Many spiritually bankrupt churches have not had a victory in years, and even the slightest victory challenges the belief that *"we're just a small church and could never do that!"* It doesn't matter how simple these victories might be as long as it is something the church has not been able to do for some time.

Passion—Spiritually alive leaders begin to realize time is of the essence as people live and die without Christ. The new vision instills a passion and urgency that was present in the beginning years of the church. This passion always stems from how the pastor and the growing group of gathered leaders model the Great Commission. Pastors need to know one thing: in the early stages of turnaround if you are not spending most of your time with the unchurched, your church doesn't have a chance of becoming spiritually alive again.

Change—The second year of turnaround, one of two things must happen: either the old guard leadership have been transformed or they are replaced by the new guard the pastor has been training for the past year. Then the growing number of spiritual leaders initiate a major change that rocks the status quo and leads to growth. The type of change is strategically important to the success of turnaround. To see what this change might be in your situation, I refer you to my book *Unfreezing Moves*.[1]

Excitement about the future—Spiritual leaders begin listening to God and are becoming more comfortable with taking risks. It's not uncommon at this point that major changes are made in the way the church is organized so that form follows function and people are allowed more freedom in beginning new ministries. But keep in mind that changing the structure without first changing the hearts of the people doesn't work.

A culture of courage—Leaders realize that in Christ they can do all things, and the pace of the turnaround hastens and worship attendance begins to increase. The leaders become living proof that perfect love does cast out all fear. New people are encouraged and nurtured by being around the leaders and the church becomes an incubator of faith—that is, a place where strangers are welcomed and nurtured in a loving environment. Decisions begin to be made on a much faster basis, and congregational or representative rule slowly shifts back to the staff making the day-to-day decisions and the board holding them accountable.

Growing leaders—All through the process the pastor has been increasing the numbers of spiritual leaders till the number reaches the tipping point where they outnumber the old guard who are not willing to grow in Christ, and it becomes impossible to stop the turnaround.

Explosion of growth—Growth feeds on growth, the minds of church leaders shift from addition to multiplication, the church moves forward on momentum alone, and the turnaround is complete.

This entire process can take as long as three to five years depending on how spiritually dead the church is in the beginning. And the process usually begins in the first year of a new pastor. Either the church has received a new pastor, or the present pastor has a transforming change.

Of course, no resurrection happens exactly like what is suggested in this chapter. But you get the drift. How will turnaround be played out in your church? Rest assured it will be a spiritual issue.

Reflection Time

Which of the above lists best describe your church?

Note

1. Bill Easum, *Unfreezing Moves* (Abingdon Press, 2002).

CHAPTER FOUR

Turnaround Is an Eternal Issue

This book is going to make some of my good friends madder than Hell. I don't mean for that to happen, but I know it's going to, so let me apologize in advance. I don't mean any disrespect. I just want to tell it like I see it. I have that right, and hopefully we can still be friends. My guess is the madder you get, the more likely it is you've put your finger on the pulse of your church's problem.

What You Believe Determines the Results

Something that is seldom talked about openly in established church circles is the difference in basic beliefs between those leaders who grow great churches and those folks content to spend their entire lives tending to the needs of struggling churches.

The vast majority of leaders in thriving churches have a belief system that emphasizes three key passions: the need for all people to find salvation through Jesus Christ; the need for all Christians to continually seek and be obedient to God's will; and a commitment to the kingdom of God. For these folks, sharing Jesus Christ with a world in spiritual peril is at the forefront of their mission in life.

On the other hand, the vast majority of leaders in struggling churches have a belief system that sees many ways to salvation; relies heavily on representative democracy and consensus; and focuses on the institutional church. For these folks doing good and following the Great Commandment is at the forefront of their mission in life. Obviously, nothing is wrong with following the Great Commandment. The problem begins when they allow mission to end with the Great Commandment and don't follow up with the Great Commission, which was Jesus' last will and testament.

Don't make the mistake of thinking these comparisons are merely replays of the old battle of the fundamentalist/evangelical versus liberal/progressive. They are far more than that—they reach into the heart of what's wrong with much of established, Western Protestantism. The belief systems of most leaders in most struggling churches result in churches that have little passion for introducing people to Christ.

Thriving Churches	Struggling Churches
Salvation only through Jesus Christ	Many Ways to God
Seek and Be Obedient to God's Will	Democracy and Consensus
Committed to Kingdom	Committed to Institutional Church
Christianity Is a Life-and-Death Matter	Christianity Is a Good Way of Life

I know these comparisons might seem a bit oversimplified, but nevertheless that is what I've experienced. And the results of the differences between these two types of leaders are phenomenal. Let's take a look at what happens.

When Jesus Isn't the Only Answer

"Jesus answered, 'I am the way and the truth and the life. No one comes to the Father except through me'" (John 14:6).

Many churches have removed Jesus from their vocabulary or have replaced him with some program or doctrine. The personal dimension of a relationship with Jesus is telescoped into a doctrinal assent. Jesus is nothing more than a correct articulation of a denomination's doctrine.

In the early years of my consulting ministry I spent a lot of time working in declining churches. After consulting in one of these churches, the pastor drove me to the airport. Just as I was getting out of the car he asked me: "You've said a lot about a personal relationship with Jesus Christ. What do you mean by that?" I was speechless. I had come face to face with the primary reason his church was struggling, and I understood why every church he had pastored had also struggled to survive.

When was the last time you wept over the spiritual condition of your city? I mean really wept. I'm not talking about being concerned about the economic or political mess it might be in. I'm talking about losing sleep because people are living and dying without knowing Jesus Christ. Yes, all of the people in your city, not just the Christians. Even the Muslims!

For the vast majority of leaders in thriving churches, having a personal relationship with Jesus Christ is a life-and-death issue. That is the well from which *all* real passion and courage springs.

But when you remove Jesus as the only hope of the world, you misdirect any passion a person might have. Instead of passion being focused on people's salvation it's focused on issues like health, education, good works, or morals. While these are important issues, they are nothing as gut-wrenching as passionately trying to save someone from an eternal destiny without God.

A small, sleepy congregation I know in Texas was averaging around 140 people in worship when a new pastor arrived with a new vision. Nineteen months later the church was running 290 in worship. What happened? Listen to what the pastor says: "We talk about Jesus. All the time. We put a lighthearted ban on talking about 'God' for everyone leading worship. We named him Jesus. We started a kangaroo court in staff meetings. Every generic 'God' comment gets fined. We laugh at each other a lot."

The pastor understands the spiritual dimension involved in turnaround for a congregation: Jesus must be the center of our passion, not some generic notion of God. In the Old Testament it was the God of Abraham, Isaac, and Jacob. In the New Testament it's the God of Jesus Christ.

> **Leaders who do not believe that Jesus Christ is the hope of the world usually do not have the passion nor feel the urgency needed to turn a church around.**

I've struggled with what has been called the "scandal of particularity" my entire ministry. It bothers me to believe that God would localize salvation in one solitary person. But that's what the Scriptures plainly say. There's no way of getting around that without gutting the Scriptures. I've looked for a loophole. None exists. Even today, I prefer to talk about the tragedy of people living and dying without knowing Jesus, rather than to even get near the subject of eternal significance. In my mind they haven't even lived if Jesus has not been their Savior and Lord. Deep down in my heart, I know the truth of the matter—without Jesus people are in serious trouble. Believing that is the only reason I would ever consider giving my entire life to the ministry of Christ. Not believing it is why so many pastors and leaders can spend all of their time in struggling churches playing nursemaid to a bunch of spiritual pygmies. They have no sense of urgency to share the good news. They don't believe people's eternal destiny hangs in the balance. Since Jesus isn't the only hope of the world, Christianity to them is a way of living morally rather than a life-and-death issue. There's nothing wrong with moral living; it should be the outcome of any legitimate faith. But moral living is not why Jesus died. Jesus died to save everyone from their sin. To not believe that guts any form of urgency to give one's life to spread the good news.

So the average pastor today drifts through life doing whatever a congregation asks him or her to do. Urgency is lost; pastoral care wins the day—forget about the Kingdom.

Reflection Time

- What would have to change in the way you go about leading if you decided to end every action, meeting, or worship service with this question: "How will this help bring people to Christ, and who is ready to commit to Jesus or to join him on the road to mission?"
- Spend time meditating on the following texts and how they have or could affect your mission in life. "Jesus answered, 'I am the way, and the truth, and the life. No one comes to the Father except through me'" (John 14:6 NIV).
- When Jesus spoke again to the people, he said, "I am the light of the world. Whoever follows me will never walk in darkness, but will have the light of life" (John 8:12).

CHAPTER FIVE

Leaders: It's Time to Die to Yourself

I have been crucified with Christ and I no longer live, but Christ lives in me. The life I live in the body, I live by faith in the Son of God, who loved me and gave himself for me. (Galatians 2:20 NIV)

So here's the rub. Before a second resurrection can occur leaders must die to themselves. That's right. Every leader needs to put Christ first and their petty desires second. That's not easy to do, and those who can't do it need to get out of the way for those who can.

My experience is that new Christians are the ones most willing to die to themselves. The problem is most leaders aren't personally making disciples, so spiritually dead churches don't have any new Christians. (When was the last time you led someone to Christ?) Instead of dying to themselves, they prefer to offer excuses as to why their churches can't grow. So, for resurrection of the church to happen, leaders must die to themselves and get on with the Great Commission. Anything short of that and forget the turnaround.

Leaders must put aside their cultural prejudices and tastes and see the bigger picture. They must fall in love with the Kingdom movement of God in the world rather than work for the survival of their church. That's right. The second resurrection begins when all of the leaders are willing to let their church die and trust God to resurrect it. That's when it is resurrected as God's church!

You see, members of a church are supposed to understand that becoming a Christian means being willing to die to oneself and to live on behalf of those who have yet to hear the good news. This means that the church must be a training ground for missionaries rather than an entitlement program for the existing members.

A Word to the Pastor

Every church resurrection I've seen begins with a new pastor. That pastor can be someone else—or it can be you, brought to new life. If you are going to expect a congregation to die to its old perspectives and behaviors, first you have to do so yourself. This may be a gut-wrenching experience for you. It may go beyond the bounds of your determination or even the limits of your faith. You may be tested sorely. It all depends on how badly you want resurrection to happen. If you believe passionately that Jesus is people's only hope, you have a much better chance of leading the turnaround.

In his book *Waking to God's Dream*[1] Bishop Dick Wills, then pastor of Christ United Methodist Church in Ft. Lauderdale, Florida, tells the story of his personal resurrection during a trip to South Africa. It's a story worth reading. Upon reflecting on his trip, he said to me, "I saw people who had nothing, but had everything." He was referring to the joy and hope they had due to their deep relationship to Jesus Christ and to one another.

He returned to his church where he had been the pastor for five years, during which time it had been slowly declining, and began living as a servant of Christ among them. It didn't take long for his people to recognize the change in his life. In time they began to ask him what had happened to him. When he told them what happened to him in South Africa, they began to ask how they could have such an experience, and the turnaround began. What Dick couldn't do in five years, the Holy Spirit accomplished in one blink of an eye.

A Word to All Leaders

So, leader, it's time to decide where you stand with Jesus. Is Jesus the hope of the world? Do you weep over people's spiritual condition? If not, let the Holy Spirit guide you to a personal relationship with Jesus. Open your heart right now and pray, "Lord Jesus, I'm sorry for how I've lived my life to this point. I want you to be the Savior and Lord of my life. I give you my commitment, my obedience, my life. Redeem all of me." If you have prayed this prayer and feel snatched from the jaws of Hell, share your story with me at easum@easumbandy.com. Hearing such stories is what my life thrives on.

A Personal Word

I first wrote about my personal story in my book *Leadership on the OtherSide*, so I'll be brief. I didn't grow up in the church. Bible stories weren't part of our home. I was introduced to Jesus on the golf course by a pastor who cared deeply about my eternal condition. I actually began the Christian journey at the age of sixteen and a half on the third hole of Hancock Golf Course in Austin, Texas. When I gave my life to Christ I was a loner, loser, D-average student, and a drunk. I had one ambition in life—to get laid and be a professional golfer. But all that changed that day. It was like taking a U-turn in the road. I actually felt as if I was snatched from the jaws of Hell and set on a course over which I had no control (I'm sure Freud would have a field day with this paragraph).

Six months later I felt the call to preach to those who had not heard the good news and to help build the Kingdom. I surrendered my life to that call and began preaching on the streets, in flop-house missions, or wherever I could find an audience. I was ordained around my twentieth birthday and began pastoring before I finished seminary. Even during seminary, my primary goal was to bring people to Jesus. All I knew was I passionately wanted others to experience the freedom and joy I had felt ever since that day on the third hole. Since that day, everything in my life has been driven by one question: How can I help fulfill the Great Commission? I hope you can say this. The more you can, the more likely you are to be able to lead the resurrection of your church.

In time I was introduced to mainline Protestantism, and I met pastors and laity who weren't passionate about fulfilling the Great Commission. Some even doubted if it was binding on us today. Others doubted whether or not Jesus is the Savior of the world. I wanted people to know Jesus so badly that I fought my entire ministry to avoid the institutional traps of mainline Protestantism and became considered by many a thorn in their flesh. But every church I pastored grew because I focused on the salvation of people—not the growth of the church.

But guess what? Over the years many people without passion have responded to my diatribes by reevaluating their commitment to the church, submitted to the Lordship of Jesus Christ, and have been set on fire for Jesus. That is what I pray will happen to you in the course of this book.

Reflection Time

- Have you totally submitted your life to Jesus Christ? If not, what's holding you back?
- Is your theology getting in the way of being on the road to mission with Jesus? If so, which is most important—to be politically correct in your doctrine or bring people to Christ?
- How did you respond to Dick Wills's story? Did you see yourself in it? Are you serving the church or Jesus Christ in the midst of the church?

Note

1. Richard Wills, *Waking to God's Dream: Spiritual Leadership and Church Renewal* (Nashville: Abingdon Press, 1999).

CHAPTER SIX

A Life Worth Watching

Then he said to them all: "If anyone would come after me, he must deny himself and take up his cross daily and follow me."
(Luke 9:23 NIV)

In the first few centuries, before the canonizing of the Scriptures, people relied on the inner character of their leaders to determine the truth of what they taught. They had the Old Testament, and before long they had the Gospels. Still, for answers to many of their issues they turned to leaders who had been taught by Jesus or taught by someone Jesus had taught. Their primary concern was whether their teachers had been actual disciples of Jesus or had been taught by a disciple of Jesus. They determined the integrity of what their teachers were saying by how it compared to what Jesus originally taught. They were as concerned with who was teaching them as with what they were being taught. Their desire was to experience Jesus, their Lord, through their teacher. It was not enough to merely hear about him; they wanted to include his essence in their daily lives.

> **Hint: Spiritual giants are grown through watching how their leaders live, not by taking a course. You are the curriculum.**

Jesus: A Life Worth Watching

The desire of the early Christians to experience and include Jesus in their daily lives explains why the very first Christian creed was "Jesus Christ is Lord."[1] Clearly, the earliest Christians considered Jesus to be the object of their love, devotion, and life itself.

The best way they knew to incorporate his teachings into their lives was by remembering how he lived and trying to reproduce it. Christianity was about a relationship, not a set of propositions or doctrines. They saw in Jesus a life worth watching. Thus, Christians were first called "followers of the Way."[2] The goal of Christianity was never about learning or teaching the Scriptures. It was about living like Jesus lived.

Followers of the Way

The earliest Jewish followers of Jesus of Nazareth referred to themselves as "followers of the Way" before they became known as Christians. The term "followers of the Way" is used twice in the Book of Acts (Acts 22:4 and 24:14). In the same way, Christianity was referred to as "the Way" six times in the New Testament (Acts 9:2, 19:9, 19:23, 22:4, 24:14, 24:22). Even Paul considered himself a follower of "the Way" (Acts 24:14).

Jesus called himself "the Way." Countless times the Scriptures record him as calling his disciples to "follow him" and learn his ways. He had the disciples hang out with him so they could see how he lived, how he thought, and how he related to God and others. In essence they were learning a trade—to be like Jesus.

The same is true today. Jesus is "the Way" and we are to follow him. We are expected to learn and emulate his ways. He is the subject of all that we do.

Such an understanding of Christianity was natural since the primary way Jesus taught was by example. Today, we call what

Jesus did mentoring. Jesus spent most of his ministry mentoring the small circle of disciples. He invited them to "come and see" how he lived. He brought them into his life, served as a role model, and taught by demonstration. He was more concerned with their inner character than with their cognitive learning. His goal was to raise up a band of disciples who studied his life in order to live it, not learn it.

One of life's most important questions might be asked at this point: are we living so close to Jesus that if we invite someone to "come and see," they will actually see Jesus in us? Are our lives worth watching?

A Major Shift in Faith

After the Scriptures were canonized, the emphasis shifted more to what was being taught rather than who was teaching the Scriptures. The emphasis shifted from experiencing a life worth watching to being taught about that life. After the legalization of Christianity in 362 A.D., Christians slowly began to follow the institutionalized church rather than Jesus. Devotion to the church and to Mary slowly took the place of submission to the Lordship of Jesus Christ. As time went on, the church dreamed up countless numbers of ways to tie the people more to the church than to Jesus. In time people began to "go to church" rather than to be on the way with Jesus.

By the end of the great councils (fifth century), the primal creed "Jesus is Lord" was replaced by two dominant creeds, The Apostles' and Nicene Creeds, both of which take an academic theological degree to comprehend. No one had to teach what it meant to call Jesus Lord, but everyone had to be taught what was meant by these two creeds.

After the Reformation, Jesus was removed even further from the daily experiences of Christians, because Christians became known as "people of the book" instead of "followers of the Way." Christianity became something to be studied rather than someone to be lived. Since that time, much of Christian history consists of battles over how to interpret "The Book" rather than on how to live as Jesus lived. Education took the place of discipling and mentoring.

Today, too many people do not believe that the words of Jesus are to be taken literally, much less that Jesus wants to be an active part of every aspect of our lives. Most churches place more emphasis on cognitive learning than on being mentored by this "life worth watching." Christians are more polarized over how to interpret Scripture than how much time they need to spend in communion with God through Christ. Perhaps this is why the morals of professing Christians seem to be no different from those of non-Christians.

Consider this quote from Rudolf Bultmann, one of the major shapers of the theology of the first half of the twentieth century:

> It is impossible to use the electric light bulb and the wireless and to avail ourselves of modern medical and surgical discoveries, and at the same time to believe in the New Testament world of spirits and miracles.[3]

This kind of thinking destroys the essence of Christianity and reduces it to little more than a set of morals by which we can achieve a "good life" and feel good about ourselves without even considering the "life worth watching." In no way does it proclaim a vision of a new Kingdom way of living and relating to God that is worth obedience and even death.

It's time we get back to following Jesus rather than the Book! That's right. "The Book" is part of our problem. We study it instead of studying Jesus. We do Bible drills instead of drilling deeper into our relationship with Jesus. For many, the Bible has become a substitute for a personal relationship with Jesus. We memorize the Bible and wouldn't know Jesus if he bit us. We've drifted far away from the "first love" of the early Christians. It's time we returned.

Of course, we need to study the Bible. But what we need to do is focus on how the Bible reveals Jesus to us and the implications of that revelation on our lives. Our focus should be more on growing our relationship with Jesus than on learning the Bible. The question becomes: *Is my life worth watching?*

What Then Can We Say?

What can we say then? Was Jesus a fool for dying for us? Or do we go the whole nine yards and say that he really wasn't resurrected and that Christianity is at best a grand story and at worst a lie? Were the first-century Christians victims of the greatest illusion of all time? Not much of a life worth watching, is it?

No, if Christianity is ever to regain its power to transform human beings and resurrect dead churches, it must return to the essence of its being—Jesus, a life worth watching. Jesus must become not only our Lord but also our mentor. We must again become students of the Way.

Whose Disciple Are You?

Everyone is someone's disciple. Someone has taught us how to live. It may be our parents or our peers, but we are someone's apprentice. The world wants us to believe we are "our own person," but not so—at least not for Christians. Christians, by definition, are disciples of Jesus. It's time we quit just talking about God and become apprentices of Jesus.

Perhaps it's also time we begin inquiring into the inner life of those who teach and lead us. Do they have a life worth watching? By watching them are we reminded of Jesus, or are they distracting us from being his apprentice? Do their actions reflect those of Jesus or of a more demented spirit? It's time we quit allowing Jesus to be watered down to the "Christ of Faith" so that there is no longer a normal, human life worth watching. It's time to put Jesus, not Christ, at the center of our apprenticeship.

Perhaps it's also time to ask ourselves, is ours a life worth watching? Are we students of Jesus? Do we have disciples who have signed on as our apprentices? And are we mentoring them in the Way?

So What Is a Life Worth Watching?

The only way to answer this question is to take a good hard look at the life of Jesus—how he lived and what he said—before he was elevated to the "Christ of Faith." I have always found it interesting and telling that those who believe more in teaching about than in demonstrating the faith find comfort in the "Christ of Faith" more than in the redemptive power of the historical Jesus. They tell us we must forget the Jesus who died for our sins and concentrate on the "Christ of Faith." That is where we will find the power to live the Godlike life. Not so! Becoming an apprentice to the life of Jesus of Nazareth is what changes us and the world!

We must believe equally in the Christ of faith and the redemptive life of Jesus. We must know both the historical Jesus and the Christ of faith. The actual Jesus of history is the bedrock of our faith in the Lordship of Christ. The Christ of faith needed to be incarnate in one who lived and died as we do. The historical Jesus is essential to understand the Christ of faith. Salvation was made possible by the Cross and Resurrection, but first of all the Incarnation had to make the Cross real. Those who know the Christ of faith know all that is needed for salvation, but they lack the human dimension for living as he did. The life of Jesus models how we should live, and his teaching illustrates what we should believe.

The redemptive life of Jesus is our guide to how Christians are supposed to live in any age. Attempting to follow the life and character of Jesus was the goal of early Christianity. Such a goal goes far beyond the popular phrase today, "What would Jesus do?" When faced with a decision, the early Christians didn't have to stop and ask this question. They were so immersed in Jesus they intuitively knew how to act. The early Christians weren't as much concerned about how they should act in response to a particular something as they were about the character of the totality of their life. Sure, they were concerned about how they reacted to the things life sent their way, but they were more concerned about living in such a way that their entire existence demonstrated what it meant to be a follower of Jesus. They knew their actions spoke louder than words. They knew that changing the inner character of a person is what Jesus was all about. They knew that salvation went to the very core of a person and changed not only what they believed but how they lived.

And where do we find the clearest picture of a life worth watching? Matthew 5–7, otherwise known as the Sermon on the Mount. I don't have time to do justice to this text, so I will point you to the most remarkable discourse on its meaning I've ever read—*The Divine Conspiracy* by Dallas Willard. He urges us to take this passage as one long sermon instead of a collection of laws or morals on how to live. He concludes that the message culminates in the statement, "Repent, for life in the Kingdom is now one of your options."[4] He places the Beatitudes within the context of the common people around him, so that when Jesus utters the Beatitudes he is not giving laws for living as much as a welcome into the Kingdom of God of all of those mentioned in the Beatitudes.

So a life worth watching is a life that welcomes and enfolds everyone, no matter how wretched or vile, into the *agape* love of God and bids them come and be an apprentice of Jesus.

Are you a student of this "life worth watching"? Do you have apprentices who are studying the life of Jesus in you? If so, how you live is as important as what you teach.

Reflection Time

- Who are you following—Jesus or the church or your doctrine or your denomination or (you fill in the blank)?
- Is your life worth watching? Are you trying to be a model of Jesus to those around you? If not, what do you need to change?
- What would happen if every leader in your church decided to end every action, meeting, worship, whatever with one of these questions: "If we do this, does it have the potential to bring someone to Christ?" or "Who is ready to commit to Jesus or to be on the road to mission with Jesus?"

Notes

1. See the following passages:
   Acts 2:36: "Therefore let all Israel be assured of this: God has made this Jesus, whom you crucified, both Lord and Christ."
   Acts 10:36: "You know the message God sent to the people of Israel, telling the good news of peace through Jesus Christ, who is Lord of all." Romans 5:11: "Not only is this so, but we also rejoice in God through our Lord Jesus Christ, through whom we have now received reconciliation." Romans 6:23: "For the wages of sin is death, but the gift of God is eternal life in Christ Jesus our Lord."
   Romans 8:39: "Neither height nor depth, nor anything else in all

creation, will be able to separate us from the love of God that is in Christ Jesus our Lord."

1 Corinthians 1:9: "God, who has called you into fellowship with his Son Jesus Christ our Lord, is faithful."

1 Corinthians 4:17: "For this reason I am sending to you Timothy, my son whom I love, who is faithful in the Lord. He will remind you of my way of life in Christ Jesus, which agrees with what I teach everywhere in every church."

1 Corinthians 6:11: "And that is what some of you were. But you were washed, you were sanctified, you were justified in the name of the Lord Jesus Christ and by the Spirit of our God."

1 Corinthians 8:6: "Yet for us there is but one God, the Father, from whom all things came and for whom we live; and there is but one Lord, Jesus Christ, through whom all things came and through whom we live."

Philippians 2:11: "And every tongue confess that Jesus Christ is Lord, to the glory of God the Father."

2. Acts 9:2.

3. *Kerygma and Myth* (London: S.P.C.K., 1957).

4. Dallas Willard, *The Divine Conspiracy* (San Francisco: Harper Collins, 1997), p. 133.

CHAPTER SEVEN

Resurrection Begins with You

*To them God has chosen to make known among the Gentiles the glorious
riches of this mystery, which is Christ in you, the hope of glory.*
(Colossians 1:27 NIV)

So, the painful truth is out: any successful turnaround begins
with *you*, whether you're a pastor or layperson. Your church
must see the resurrected life of Christ in you. Christ in you is the
hope of the church. That is where resurrection begins. *You* can't
resurrect the church, but *Christ* in you can.

You Are the Curriculum

People are always asking me what I think is the best resource
for turning around a church. My response often takes them
aback. "You are," I tell them. "You are the curriculum for the
turnaround. What your church sees you willing to do says more
than all the curriculum you can buy."

So what does it mean to be the curriculum? It means at least
the following: the turnaround of your church begins when the
following traits guide you and your church.

Being Obedient to God's Commands

"And this is love: that we walk in obedience to his commands.
As you have heard from the beginning, his command is that you
walk in love" (2 John 1:6, NIV).

"Because of the service by which you have proved yourselves, men will praise God for the obedience that accompanies your confession of the gospel of Christ" (2 Cor. 9:13).

Not much is heard about obedience in dying churches these days. Instead, a lot is heard about duty. They aren't the same. Obedience grows out of our growing relationship with God through Jesus Christ and fills the church with love; duty grows out of a sense of guilt and fills the church with control. When people are driven by duty they do things simply because someone twists their arm even if it doesn't bring meaning to their life. When people are driven by obedience to God's commands, they only do those things that bring honor to God. Their obedience is to the gospel, not Robert's Rules of Order or a church constitution. God doesn't honor churches riddled with guilt and duty. God honors those who are obedient to God's commands.

In other words, God prefers to work with our weakness. God wants us to acknowledge that our source of power resides in our growing relationship with Jesus Christ. The more obedient we are to him, the more spiritual power we have. Not because we are worthy, but because God is working through us to achieve the ultimate goals—the Great Commission and the Great Commandment.

Leader, submit yourself to the Lordship of Jesus Christ. Do what Christ did. Because Christ humbled himself and became obedient unto death, God exalted him. This obedience of Christ, which was so pleasing to God, must become the heart and soul of our Christian walk. Just as a servant knows to obey his or her master in all things, so our surrender to an implicit and unquestioning obedience must become the essential characteristic of our lives.

Leader, if you want to resurrect your church, lose control of your life to Christ. Submit to his Lordship. Don't just play church. Get serious, if you want your church to have the future

God desires for it. Demonstrate to your church things are going to be different in your life and see what God will do.

Now you are beginning to see that turnaround requires far more than mere gimmicks or new programs.

Living by Faith

But my righteous one will live by faith.
And if he shrinks back,
I will not be pleased with him. (Heb. 10:38)

Church leaders are always telling me *why* they can't do something. I guess they never read Philippians 4:13, which clearly says, "I can do everything through him who gives me strength." Do you believe that? Resurrection begins the moment you truly believe that with all your heart.

If you want people to believe in the resurrection of your church, you must believe in the power of God to work through you and to give you the strength to pull it off through God's guidance. Turnaround is hard, messy business. So messy that most pastors who try will lose their jobs because they try to do it on their own strength. Remember, Christ in you is the hope of your church.

Living by faith means being willing to take risks, trying things you've never tried, and going places you've never been. It means stepping out beyond your comfort level and taking people with you on the journey.

But have you noticed most church leaders lead like scared rabbits, afraid to take risks, always looking for the cheapest, easiest way out of whatever mess their church is in? They are filled with fear either because they are afraid of losing the status quo, losing control of how things are done, or losing their job. All of these responses show a lack of faith. Faith is about change and spontaneous movements of the Spirit. Faith flies in the face of status quo and control. Faith isn't afraid to take risks!

How did church leaders become so fearful? The answer is simple—when Jesus isn't our first love we learn to reward fear. Ever notice how church boards usually acquiesce to the person who has the greatest objection to whatever is being proposed? It's as if the person with the most fear is the one who is rewarded the most.

Most church leaders today are simply afraid to risk. They lack courage. They've hunkered down in the bunker, burying their heads in the sand as if doing nothing about their condition will solve their problem. It's not that they don't care about their churches—they do. Some deeply care about the plight of their churches. The problem is their relationship with Christ has not grown to the point that they understand that Christ in them is the hope of their churches. The lack of such a relationship renders them too afraid to take the necessary action.

Living by faith takes courage—the kind of courage that only faith in Christ can produce. A lack of courage feeds on the presence of fear. So, one of the first tasks of the turnaround pastor is not to try to motivate church leaders but to take them deeper into their relationship with the one who takes away all fear—Jesus. Remember the text: "There is no fear in love. But perfect love drives out fear, because fear has to do with punishment. The one who fears is not made perfect in love" (1 John 4:18 NIV).

If you understand the problem not as a lack of interest, but rather as a lack of courage, you begin to interpret the dying church and your potential response in a whole different light. Your task is not to get their attention, motivate, or pique their interest, but to help them find courage somewhere in their hearts and minds. The only way to do so is for them to fully give themselves to the Lordship of Jesus Christ—the one who casts out all fear.

Living by faith isn't easy. For most turnaround churches it means being willing to spend all of the rainy-day money in one big attempt to turn the ship around. Spiritually deep people don't look at their budgets to see how little they can spend; they look at their budgets to see if how they are spending money is bringing people to Christ. When God moves in their hearts to do something, they don't ask if they can afford it; they trust God to supply the funds!

For turnaround pastors, living by faith always means risking their salary and job on something they know has to happen for the turnaround to begin. It may mean confronting a bully who has kept the church hostage for years. It may mean doing without salary so that the mission can be accomplished. It may mean leading the church into something totally new without any guarantee it will work.

My first year at the church I resurrected was the worst year of my life. I didn't get paid. People were standing in line to have me removed. Half of the people left during the first six months. My denomination wouldn't help. It was a mess. All we had was our faith, nothing more.

Feeding on Prayer

"He said to them, 'My house will be called a house of prayer,' but you are making it a 'den of robbers'" (Matt. 21:13 NIV).

In most books on turnaround, the importance of prayer is understated. I don't want to make that mistake. My interviews with the pastors of successful turnarounds always reveal the importance prayer played. Without it these pastors would not have kept their sanity during the ordeal. Notice the words "sanity" and "ordeal." Turnaround takes its toll on everyone. Pastors lose their jobs, and laypeople lose their friends. Neither is easy.

So prayer becomes your primary source of power. The best way to draw closer to Jesus Christ, the one who will do the resurrection, is by having a solid prayer life. You need to feed on it. Drink in every moment with God you can find time for.

Notice I said "find time for." Most successful turnaround pastors set aside a certain time each day to pray and meditate. Otherwise the responsibilities of the day eat up all of your time. When asked what one of the key things they did in the turnaround of First Christian Church in Kerrville, Texas, the pastor said, "Every day at 2:00 p.m. we pray for our church to double."

In 1969, I began the turnaround of a church that was spiritually dead. My first Sunday morning I cast a vision of a thriving church with thousands of people in ministry, and I invited anyone interested to join me that night at the parsonage to dream about such a church. About a dozen potential leaders gathered that night and continued to meet every week for the next eight or nine months for Bible study, prayer, and sharing. It didn't take long to realize the turnaround was going to cause many things to get rough. People were lining up ten or twelve deep to talk to the personnel committee about getting rid of me. Longtime friends were turning on each other. One married couple separated over the events of those early months of turnaround. It was an ugly scene for eighteen months. During this time our group came face to face with the spiritual principalities and powers Paul wrote about in Ephesians.[1]

Because of that ugliness our little group realized that if the turnaround was going to happen we had to support one another in prayer, and we needed to do it every day. So we set aside a definite time every day to pray for one another. We did this so the difficulties of the moment wouldn't rob us of prayer time.

Bringing a church to life brings out the best and the worst in people. Unfortunately, the worst often gets out of control and people are not only mean-spirited but they can become downright evil. Some will go to any lengths to keep the status quo due to fear of the unknown or loss of control.

Because things will get messy during your turnaround, here's a tip on how to keep the lid on. The next time your board meeting gets heated, don't wait for it to get out of hand. Instead, fall down on your knees in front of everyone and start praying. Then watch what happens to the conflict and anger. It will go away. Even the meanest person will be shamed by your actions, and those who are on the fence will take heart. God will begin to move, and things will happen that you never dreamed possible. But your heart must be pure here. If it is a gimmick, God won't honor it.

Willing to Lead

As I said earlier, most established churches reward fear over courage. Therefore, most established churches are like a big magnet that continually draws people who like to control others as well as people who like to be controlled. Such an atmosphere is negatively charged with the wrong kind of leader and follower. Neither reaches their potential in such an environment. Fear and control stagnates spiritual growth because God's spirit can't be controlled. It must be allowed to run free and wild. Dying churches do everything they can to control the Spirit and thus quench it.

In such an environment the pastor and a few key lay leaders must find ways to take the leadership away from controlling, fearful people. Without doing so, churches never turn around. In the vast majority of cases, turnaround begins the moment two or three controlling leaders are replaced by people who are led by the Spirit rather than by fear.

Turnaround never happens unless the pastor is the spiritual and administrative leader of the church. But a problem exists. Many pastors are reluctant to assume such a leadership position.

The following is a series of emails I received on our advanced leadership forum and my responses.[2]

Subject:	Re: [Advanced Leadership] Pondering Leadership
Date:	4/13/2006 10:55:52 A.M. Central Daylight Time
From:	anyone@USA.com
To:	advancedleadership@lists.easum.com

Thanks for the discussion on leadership. What do I do in a small declining church? The cry I've heard lately is "We want leadership," so I've been told I need to play more the role of the authoritative leader or "benign dictator." I have mixed feelings about this:
1) Is this a true need or a smoke screen to shift responsibility and have someone to blame eventually?
2) Am I up to it?
3) Do I want to?

Here is my response:

Unless you play this role the church never grows. I've never seen otherwise. Jesus taught us that even people like Peter needed a leader to grow him to where he could stand on his own. Take the reins and be the leader. Live openly as Jesus lived. Serve Christ in their midst rather than serving the church. The Scriptures give you that authority as pastor. Read how the New Testament church functioned. That is the way it should function today. Take *all* of the authority they will give you and lead with integrity.

Another person on the forum responded back to the original post with this post.

I heard the same thing this past January during some listening meetings we had. When I questioned them as to what they meant by this they said, "We want you to tell us what to do." I responded with, "I'll tell you what to do, to an extent, but we're all adults here and there comes a time when you've got to take some responsibility." Their response was some mumbling then a shift of topic. . . .

I responded back with this post:

Folks, when growing spiritual giants you have to look at most adults in struggling churches as if they were infants. If they knew what to do they would do it, but they don't have a clue at the moment. At the beginning of their growth, leaders have to tell them what to do, just like infants. If you fail to do this the church will never grow. This is a basic fallacy with many pastors. Most church leaders in established churches are spiritual pygmies. You must guide them along just like children until they begin to grow. As they grow you begin to give them more responsibility. I know this may sound awful, but consider your role to be that of a spiritual parent and you will see the wisdom in this.

Toward the end of this exchange the following email was posted in response to the original message:

Have you read the book *Transforming Power* by Robert Linthicum? He points out that many Christian leaders have been afraid of power, afraid to desire power, and afraid to use power. Linthicum makes a powerful (no pun intended) argument that Godly power is not only a must but also a mandate for church leaders. We've far too long allowed ourselves to be Caspar Milquetoasts in the face of the world and those within the church who would derail the vision, mission, and values. Bill E wrote an incredible article years ago: "On Not Being Nice for the Sake of the Gospel." As he suggests, nowhere does Jesus command us to be nice. We're to be committed to following Jesus, the Jesus who said, "All power belongs to me. . . . Now you go!" We've been empowered, so long as we'll take up that mantle. Power exists, and someone is going to plug into it. The question is will it be those committed to Jesus' mission or those committed to derailing that mission? Take up the mantle, [he inserted the person's name]. Power in the hands of faithful followers is a beautifully effective God-given tool.

This last email nailed the issue—either the pastor takes up the mantle of power or someone else will. The question is whether it will be those committed to Jesus' mission or those bent on control.

I receive many emails like the original post. Many pastors are afraid of power. They have been trained to be chaplains rather than leaders. They are unsure about the biblical responsibilities of being the spiritual and administrative leader of the church. They see their role more as caregivers than as leaders. Such an understanding of the role of pastor has to change if turnaround is going to happen.

The use of power cannot be avoided in a church. It will either be prayer-filled power or power for the sake of controlling what happens. Someone will take power. No doubt about it. In the vacuum caused by the absence of a strong spiritual leader, controlling people move into the vacuum and assume leadership. Instead, the leaders ought to be the pastor and a handful of key laypeople who are committed to the kingdom of God rather than to the institutional church.

Holding on Like a Dog with a Bone

It's not unusual for turnaround to take five or more years. During the early going the stress level experienced by everyone involved can escalate to almost intolerable levels. Things can get so bad that most leaders will question the wisdom of even starting the process. Some will want to give up and let things return to what they were. It is here that the role of the pastor becomes crucial. Your role is to exemplify tenacious perseverance.

Steve Sjogren tells of his early years as planter of Cincinnati Vineyard Church. After two years of hard ministry the church was foundering, about to collapse. Even though he was devastated, Steve knew that God wanted him to plant a church in Cincinnati, so he continued on, looking for a breakthrough here and there until he stumbled on servant evangelism.[3] Today the church worships over 6,000 a Sunday. Without perseverance most churches will never turn around.

Do you remember the scene from Cecil B. DeMille's *The Ten Commandments* when the Hebrew slaves were crossing the Red Sea and were looking up at the giant columns of water on both sides? Joshua took Moses to a high rock where he could be seen by all of the people. Why? To give them the courage and hope to go on when faced with destruction all around them. This is what church leaders need from their pastors during the early stages of turnaround. They need someone whose very actions convey courage, hope, and strength.

Pastor, this means your turnaround leaders need two things from you. First, they must never see you doubting the process, even if you are filled with doubt. If you have doubts, work on them in private. Second, once you have begun the process you must never blink, even if it costs you your job. Doing so gives strength to those who relish the status quo and destroys the hopes of those who yearn for change.

Creating a Different Future

The more I listen to pastors talk about controllers, "church bullies," the inability to break through the barriers of traditions, the restraints brought about because people are more in love with fear than with Jesus, and—the most common of all—the insistence that "we've never done it that way before," the more I realize how deeply most churches are enveloped in a culture of fear. Too many church people are resigned to what is instead of passionately dreaming of what could be. It breaks my heart, and

I hope it does yours also. Well, I've got news—it doesn't have to be that way. One spiritually alive person can change all of the above.

Spiritually alive leaders deeply believe they can create a different future for their church. They know God can and will do something great through them if they put themselves in the middle of what God is already doing. They believe that, through them, God can re-create an environment around them in which people grow into spiritual giants. Such a confidence radiates out from them, grabbing those around them, helping them also believe that they can make a difference in this world.

Spiritually alive leaders create a culture of courage and help others transform from resignation to possibility. They don't achieve this change through the program of the day. They do it by becoming obedient to God's direction rather than the direction of those around them. They listen to the voice inside instead of the voice of the church board or bully. Then they take action even if it may cost them their jobs or their friends.

Hear me clearly: one spiritually alive person can bring about resurrection in a church. No singular action ever takes place without changing the course of the future. The actions of one person do make a difference. Start living from the vantage point of faith and the whole church system begins to change. Will you be the one who begins the process that leads to the resurrection of your church?

Moving On

So, if you want to turn around your church, you must realize it begins with you. You must be willing to live by faith and take the necessary risks involved in turnaround. Fear must not be allowed to control your church. You must fortify your risk-taking by regular prayer. You must be willing to be the spiritual leader and not allow bullies to control what happens in your church. You must create a culture of courage. And you must never blink in the process.

Reflection Time

- Describe your obedience to Christ. Where can you deepen the obedience? What corners of your life have you kept to yourself?
- Are you willing to take risks even if you're not sure of the outcome? If not, what's getting in the way?
- Is your prayer life a source of constant strength? If not, how can you make it so?
- Set aside a specific time each day for prayer, meditation, and reflection on your ministry. Don't let anything distract you from this time.
- Pastor, are you afraid to exercise power? If so, why? What do you need to do to change that attitude?
- Do you fully understand that you are the curriculum in any successful turnaround?

Notes

1. "For our struggle is not against flesh and blood, but against the rulers, against the authorities, against the powers of this dark world and against the spiritual forces of evil in the heavenly realms" (Eph. 6:12).

2. Go to www.easumbandy.com/store/registrations/join_the_eba_ community to subscribe.

3. http://servantevangelism.com/

CHAPTER EIGHT

Rolling Away the Stone

Earlier I made a comment about the difficulty and messiness of turnaround. Three out of four pastors who attempt it lose their job. But turnaround doesn't have to be that way. So, this chapter offers pointers on how to accomplish resurrection without being the object of crucifixion.

Don't Ask for Permission

No one wants to be told they're spiritually dead. So, pastor, you and your group will never receive permission to lead a church through this kind of change. Instead of asking for permission you must decide if you are spiritually up to the challenge. If so, begin the process. If not, take your Bible and go off, and don't return until God has laid a vision on you. Then begin the process or get out of ministry.

So Where Do I Begin?

Okay, pastor, if you've decided your spiritual life is up to the task, the first action you must take is to cast a vision of a different future and gather a group whose eyes light up over the vision. Everything else in the turnaround depends on this first step. Most spiritually dead churches are filled with good people who have no clue about the gospel. Their vision of the church is stunted. They have little or no concept of the marvelous things

God is doing throughout the world. It is up to you to cast so clear a vision of a New Testament church that they can't help but react to it.

Gather Your Group

Jesus couldn't do what he did without a team, and neither can you. The main thing he did while he was on earth was gather and mentor a ragtag group of people who were willing to put everything on the line for what God was doing in their lives. That is the kind of group you need to gather together *before* you move the church toward resurrection.

This group may or may not presently be in the church, and they may or may not presently be the formal leadership of the church. The more of them presently in leadership, the less blood will be shed. So pull this group together wherever you can find them—in the church, outside the church, or in leadership.

The purpose of this time together is to embed in the small band of growing disciples the heartbeat of the gospel: Jesus is Lord and the Great Commission is the mandate of the church. The purpose is not Bible study. You are equipping these people to be the future leaders of the church.

Take whatever time it takes to gather and mentor this group in the Way. You will need to spend enough time with them for them to catch the spirit of your dream for the church.

Once your group has devoured this book, I suggest that you lead them through a study of the book of Acts. Don't go buy a study; develop it yourself around the vision you are casting. Everything you need to know about turnaround is in Acts. In the appendix you will find a series of articles on the preaching I did from the book of Acts the first year of my turnaround experience.

Two commitments are needed from this group. First, pastor, you must commit to spending at least 80 percent of your time and energy rolling away the stone, even if it costs you your job. Resurrection is never easy; it cost the disciples their lives. It may cost yours as well. But the point is—make a commitment to see this through no matter what. Too much is at stake here for you to begin the process and bail out when the going gets tough, and it will.

I suggest that part of your mentoring is actually going out into the community and bringing people to Christ. The smaller the church the more important this suggestion is. If you're in a small church (under 300 in worship) and you personally are responsible for bringing 50 new people into the church, you will create a buzz as well as give inspiration to the group you are mentoring.

Second, the group needs to make the commitment to put the resurrection before everything else, even if it costs them some friends—and it probably will. Resurrections never happen without losing some people along the way. This group needs to understand that turnaround is spiritual warfare, and things may get messy, and they have to stand firm and not leave you hanging out to dry.

I know. These last two paragraphs don't sound very encouraging. But everyone needs to know that resurrection is a spiritual thing, and spiritual things bring out either the best or the worst in people. Some people are going to get madder than Hell and do unbelievably bad things before it is all over. You just need to be prepared for it and respond in love.

Now, the nasty news: those who allowed the church to get in the present mess are not the ones who will lead the church back to spiritual health. The present leaders of the church must either be replaced or die to themselves and be resurrected spiritually.

So, pastor, you are faced with a choice: either you need to effect a coup with a new group you gather around you and replace all of your present leaders, or God must resurrect your present leadership. You will have less bloodshed if you can avoid the coup, but it will take longer.

Either way, when you cast your vision, watch to see whose eyes light up, and gather them together in a small group who will become the turnaround leaders in a few months. Ask them to covenant with you to meet weekly for several months to discern what God has in store for your church. Doing so will invoke the Gideon principle—you will dwindle the group down to those who are ready to put Jesus before anything else.

I also suggest you consider how the following can be augmented into your time together with this group.

- Bible study designed around spiritual growth and leadership development.

- Teaching and mentoring personal and corporate prayer.

- Simply hanging out with those who are ready to go deeper and intentionally mentoring them to become confident leaders in the church.

- Journaling and the sharing of life's issues with a group of fellow travelers.

- Small groups that focus on life application and multiplication of leadership.

- Participation in ministry in which people's lives are changed through the act of serving one another.

An excellent book for busy people is *High-Voltage Spirituality* by Bill Tenny-Brittian.[1] An excellent video is "Spiritual Disciplines for Ordinary People" with John and Nancy Ortberg.[2]

The Coup

The turnaround will hopefully involve the spiritual transformation of your present leaders. But if that is not the case, and you need to effect a coup, do so the second year of your tenure.

Every church has a different polity system, so you will have to decide where, when, and how the coup should take place. You want to ensure that whatever you do, you replace those who hold the financial purse strings, make the big decisions, and decide whether the pastor stays or goes. Making this move may also include working during the year to replace those on the nominating committee.

When Mike Slaughter became pastor of Ginghamsburg United Methodist Church in Tipp City, Ohio, in 1979, it was a quaint, dying congregation of around ninety people in worship. During his first year he preached on the character of the New Testament church and spent much of his time gathering a group of individuals whose eyes lit up when he shared his vision. He then took them deeper into the faith. The following year he fixed it so all of them were placed into office and the coup was complete. Today (2006), the church worships some 4,800 people, including children.

Now, if you're feeling queasy, remember that what you are about is a battle for the heart and soul of every person in your church. Anytime God begins to move in a spiritually dead congregation, evil rears its ugly head and things begin to unravel. Good people will do bad things they never dreamed they were capable of—all to protect the status quo even if the stench is so bad they have trouble not holding their noses. Your church is held hostage by folks who have lost their way and their first love. Some could even be called spiritual terrorists! You are doing them a favor calling them back to Jesus and his mission, so don't blink here. Go ahead and plan the coup.

One Critical Mistake to Avoid

When pastors lose their job and laypeople lose their friends over attempting a turnaround, it is usually due to one thing—they are working so long and hard at turnaround that their health and faith suffer so severely that they lose their cool and make bad or hasty decisions. The one thing spiritual leaders cannot afford is to lose their cool. Leaders are the thermometer in a church. If they lose their cool and escalate the heat, the angst of the whole church is raised, and turnaround soon becomes crucifixion. Such volatility must be minimized.

The average pastor can't work sixty hours a week in a highly emotional, stress-driven environment and be effective. The average layperson has a forty-hour workweek that is stressful enough without the added stress of turnaround. So keeping the stress level at a minimum is critical. To accomplish this low stress level, leaders have to be fresh and on their toes.

So, leaders, get off of whatever treadmill the church has you on at the moment. Pastor, you don't have to make all of the hospital visits. Decide which ones you can let a layperson visit without losing your job. Layperson, you don't have to say "yes" to every committee the church offers. All turnaround leaders need to learn to say "no" and focus on the one thing that always leads to turnaround—being spiritual leaders who are always prayerfully focused on the Great Commission and the Great Commandment.

Prepare for Your Stress Points

Every turnaround will be stressful. All one has to do to verify this comment is talk with pastors who have been through the process. They will tell you it nearly ruined them, their marriage, and their faith. But it doesn't have to be that way.

Leaders and their spouses often face major stress when one or more of the following situations happen.

When controllers are pressured to leave office. We have seen very few turnarounds take place without the loss of some members.

When making the attempt either to change an existing worship service or begin an additional worship service. The easiest way to turn a church around is to begin a new worship service designed in a way that today's person can hear the gospel. However, if the leaders have little clue about the essential mission of God's church or if they prefer for the church to remain a cozy little club or family chapel, conflict erupts. If the new service succeeds, the conflict often gets worse.

When the pastor begins breaking the personal chaplain mold and begins to lead. Such action always results in a shift in emphasis. Scripture teaches that clergy equip God's people to do the ministry. Somehow the attitude in some churches is that "the laity run the church and clergy do the ministry." We see very few churches turning around where the paid staff does most or all of the ministry.

This transition also takes a lot of time. One of the best cures for opposition to lay ministry occurs when laypeople begin to experience the joy of doing ministry themselves, as well as being ministered to by equipped laity. The key is to go slowly, and seriously equip God's people for ministry. Begin the process by training new people to expect laity to minister to them instead of the paid staff's tending to their every need. Next, begin to ask, "Who among our longtime members will accept ministry from the hands of laity?" Let the laity minister to them while the pastor or staff continue to minister to those who expect you to play "pastor fetch." In time all of the ministry will be done by the laity.

When the transition begins to cost money. Most dying churches have money in the bank they've saved for a rainy day. Such passion, though often misdirected, is understandable, especially for those who lived through the Great Depression. Churches with fewer than one hundred and twenty-five people in worship need to look for ways to implement the transition with as little cost as possible.

When I first came to the church I pastored for twenty-four years, we had very few people in attendance. I launched the turnaround without spending a dime, simply by spending as much time as possible out of the office and away from the flock, but without losing the pulpit.

When a desire for high commitment begins to encroach on the entitlements usually afforded longtime members. We know that the higher the standards placed on church leaders, the healthier the church becomes. However, making this shift causes conflict. Longtime members who feel entitled to all the benefits of membership become upset when encouraged to act like servants who exist on behalf of the non-Christian people around them.

This conflict often surfaces when leaders try to rearrange the way the church spends money, targeting more of it toward non-Christians; or when paid staff begin devoting more time to non-Christians than to members; or when members are asked to park farther away from the church to make room for visitors; or when some higher standards are applied to membership and leadership. Church leaders often find that they have to "grandfather" the longtime members and apply the new standards only to the new people coming into the church—at least at first.

When new leaders make mistakes trying to implement the innovations. The opposition uses mistakes as an excuse to say, "I told you so," and begins to stir up the conflict even further. The best way to deal with this stress: admit and celebrate the mistakes as a great time for learning instead of trying to justify the failed action.

When churches with paid staff find that before the turnaround can happen, they must replace some long-term paid staff. The staff that most often have to be replaced are the longtime secretaries who refuse to use twenty-first century technology or who use their position to slow down the transition; the choir directors who try to sabotage the new worship services; or the part-time financial secretaries who tell less than the truth about the church's financial health, hoping that bad news will discourage people from starting new ministries.

Tips for Turnaround Pastors

What else can you do to handle the added stress of a turnaround ministry?

- Keep your own faith strong. Take time for regular Bible study and prayer each day. Get away from the church on a regular basis so that you have space to dream and ponder and be filled with wonder once again. Keep in mind that congregations are seldom healthier than their spiritual leaders.

- Embody servanthood in all you do before beginning the turnaround. Everything about you must scream servanthood. Go out of your way to serve those who oppose the turnaround.

- Be prepared for conflict. Some people are going to do some unbelievably unchristian things. Don't take their actions personally. You don't have this luxury. You must be the spiritual leader of the church even in the midst of conflict. If you respond personally, you raise the level of conflict beyond the ability to overcome. Instead, you must pray for the opposition. Learn from those who oppose you, but do not let them set the course for the church.

- Realize the higher your spiritual gift of mercy, the more difficult the turnaround will be for you. The gift of mercy usually means the person avoids conflict, has trouble firing ineffective people, would rather try to save a staff person than replace them, has trouble confronting mean-spirited controllers, and has difficulty making the hard decisions. Turnaround pastors are often called on to choose the mission over the interests or desires of individuals, even those close to them. People with high mercy gifts find these decisions hard to make. They also tend to take things more personally than they can afford to and still survive the turnaround. So if your mercy gift is high, consider the costs. If you decide to proceed, surround yourself with people who have low-mercy gifts.

- Keep your focus on developing spiritual giants instead of developing new programs or worship services. Focus on growing people, not the church.

- Make sure you are secure enough not to worry about job security or feeding your family. Another way to say it: if you're convinced a turnaround is what God wants you to do, then if you lose your pulpit, have confidence that God will open up another place for you to serve.

- Make sure you are in the turnaround for the long haul and aren't going to jump ship at the first sign of mutiny. To do so destroys the hope of those who want change and increases the power of those who don't want change.

- Prepare your new key leaders by not over-promising or under-preparing them. Leaders need to know what to expect *before* committing to the turnaround. They should never be surprised by the responses.

• Plan one or two quick victories, especially in the really small church. People need to have something to celebrate in the early part of the actual transition.

After all of this, the best advice is to follow the passion of your call. If you sense transition is what needs to occur, start it. If you're not sure, or if you consider it only because so many of your colleagues are doing it—forget it.

Make Sure You and Your Family Are in Order

Because turnaround can be so all-consuming, you need to take extra time during the transition to care for your soul and that of your family. Failure to heed this warning will cause regret the rest of your life. When asked what he would do different in the turnaround of Ginghamsburg Church, Mike Slaughter, pastor of Ginghamsburg, said, "I would have given much more attention to my soul and that of my family."[3]

Notes

1. Bill Tenny-Brittian, *High-Voltage Spirituality* (St. Louis: Chalice Press, 2005).

2. Available from Willow Creek Church.

3. From an interview with Mike Slaughter in early 1998.

CHAPTER NINE

Life beyond the Tomb

So, now the spiritual life of your growing group of disciples has pushed the church to the tipping point and the church is ready to move forward. What does the resurrected church look like on the other side of the tomb?

This chapter describes the basic behavior I observe in resurrected churches; it is not meant to show you how to effect the change. Every effective turnaround church I've worked with or know about has the basic characteristics I will now describe. (For those wanting the nuts and bolts of turnaround, see my book *Unfreezing Moves.*)[1]

The Four Essentials of the Resurrected Church

Resurrected congregations have figured out the four essentials of a spiritually alive, faithful church.

- Spiritually alive, faithful churches live to bring new people into relationship with Jesus and to the church (Church Leaders Have a New Focus: The Great Commission).

- Spiritually alive, faithful churches live to retain the lion's share of new people (A New Form of Worship and Assimilation Emerges).

- Spiritually alive, faithful churches live to incubate, equip, and mobilize the congregation (Growing Disciples Is Fundamental: The Great Commandment).

- Spiritually alive, faithful churches live to send disciples back out to tell their networks about Jesus and the church (Evangelism Is Contagious).

That's the essence of life beyond the tomb. Here's a brief look at the resurrected church.

Church Leaders Have a New Focus: The Great Commission

The resurrected church focuses the vast majority of its time, energy, and money on reaching those in the area who do not yet know the joy of being followers of the Way. The pastor spends more time with people outside the church than in the office or going to committees. Laypeople invite their networks to attend their church or small group and spend less time in meetings. The leadership of the church understands the importance of the first impression and does everything it can to make the first few minutes on the property a warm, welcoming experience.[2] Their goal is to make people feel more like guests in their home than visitors in a church. From the parking lot to the parking lot laypeople seek to be helpful—especially to new people.

Every decision is based on whether or not it has the potential to introduce someone to Christ or take someone deeper in their spiritual development. Ministries are in place for non-Christians and new Christians as well as maturing Christians. The church even reallocates its budget so it can effectively connect with the public through advertising. For more on advertising see my book *Go BIG: Lead Your Church to Explosive Growth.*[3]

In resurrected churches, pastors spend most of their time making sure the environment of the church is conducive to incubating new people and growing new leaders. They are no longer available to the entire church. Dying churches expect their leadership to be there for them; spiritually alive churches expect them to be there for the unchurched, the paid staff, and the key lay leaders. They spend time with those who have the capability of multiplying the ministry of the church. They function more like a spiritual midwife than a CEO. Their role is to help others birth their God-given gifts.[4] This is a hard shift to make and usually takes several years for it to be fully embraced by the old guard.

A New Spirit of Worship Emerges

The one thing I can say with no reservation (and you know how hard it is to say that these days?) is turnaround always involves either the improvement of worship or the addition of a new form of worship. Worship never expresses more faith than the faith of the community. Worship is always dead in spiritually dead churches because worship flows out of those who lead it. If the leaders are spiritually dead so is the worship. But when people's spirits are resurrected, waves of excitement and anticipation vibrate throughout not just the worship but the entire Sunday (or whatever day) experience. It's not hype or gimmicks; it's the power of God flowing through the leaders. Often you can sense it when you walk in the doors.

Churches often make the mistake of believing all they have to do is create a great contemporary worship service and the church will grow. Not so. Behind that new service must beat a spiritual drum, a desire to connect with the unchurched. The beat comes from a passion to see people find Christ. It's not the contemporary service that changes the church; it's the passion behind the creation of that service. Just like everything else, God only honors those things that are in tune with what God is doing. God isn't in the business of blessing a certain form of worship.

Hempfield United Methodist Church in Lancaster, Pennsylvania, had been on a plateau for decades in the high two hundreds in worship. A new pastor arrived who had a heart for the Great Commission. After a three-day consultation with me, he added a new worship service that was indigenous to the area, and over the next decade the church grew to over 1,100 in worship.

The relevancy of the worship experience is a fundamental key to retaining people long enough for them to begin plugging into the life of the congregation. However, keep in mind that people aren't looking for a contemporary worship service; they are looking for a contemporary church where they can experience God. They are looking for a relevant, indigenous experience, which goes way beyond just what happens during worship. The experience begins in the parking lot and spills over into everything that happens and everyone with whom they come into contact. You can have a great worship service but no spiritual power, and it won't attract and nurture people.

The vast majority of the time turnaround involves the addition of a worship service that is totally different from the existing one. How easy it is to add this service depends on the spiritual depth of the people. The more faith they have, the easier it will be. It is hard for people without a strong faith to believe in the need to add such a service when the present service isn't near its full capacity and it meets their own needs. Selfish people have difficulty praying and paying for a service they never intend to attend. But spiritual people have a faith that doesn't require proof or benefit them.

Studies have shown the time of the new service to be as important as the style. When you get the right style and time together, you have a winner. The best times are after 9:30 a.m. on Sunday.

You want to avoid having to move an existing service. But you don't have to worry about putting a new service at the same time as Sunday school since Sunday school is seldom a player in the turnaround or in the future of most churches in the twenty-first century.

However, great worship requires great methods of assimilation. If new people are left sitting in a pew for months, odds are they won't be in your church two years from now. Resurrected churches spend much of their time and energy perfecting methods of assimilating new people into the Body within the first ninety days. Every effective method of assimilation I've seen involves some form of the following six steps—identifying, inviting, equipping, deploying, coaching, and recognizing. How these steps are carried out is all over the map, so the application isn't the key to assimilation. The key is how intentional these churches are in assimilating people into the Body. As we will see later, most resurrected churches assimilate by bringing new people into small groups, but in some way the six steps are always present and used intentionally by every leader.

Growing Disciples Is Fundamental: The Great Commandment

People seldom grow in worship. That's not its role. Growing people worship to give thanks for what God has already done in and through their lives. In the vast majority of faithful churches I've worked with or know of, people grow in two primary places: in intimate small groups and in service to others.

The small groups we see working focus on three things—leadership development, multiplication of groups, and community. Bible study isn't the real issue. People grow by allowing the biblical principles to modify and shape their lives. Dead churches focus on Bible study; faithful churches focus on behavior modification. (For more on this subject see my book *Go BIG with Small Groups: Eleven Steps to An Explosive Small Group Ministry* [Nashville: Abingdon, 2006].)

In faithful churches it is normal to see a high percentage of people involved in weekly hands-on ministry to others. We have learned from missionaries abroad the sooner you involve a non-Christian in some form of hands-on ministry, the sooner that person becomes a Christian. Since North America is now one of the primary mission fields in the world, we have to act like missionaries. That means we must realize people often belong by becoming involved in ministry.

One more thing about service—when it comes to ministry, a resurrected church never, ever sees committee work as ministry. In fact, resurrected churches avoid committees and meetings like the plague, because they know no one ever becomes a Christian or grows more like Christ by being on a committee. Instead, they want as many of their people on the mission field, in the battlefield—where people are hurting, confused, and searching.

Evangelism Is Contagious

Now we've come full circle. We've seen the Alpha and the Omega of the resurrected church. Once being brought into a relationship with Jesus Christ and the church, people are equipped and sent back out into the world to be salt, light, and leaven. Faithful churches do whatever is necessary to send their people out from the church with a message that can transform their communities.

You see, faithfulness is not about holding on or surviving or even persevering; it is about being with Jesus in the mission field. Faithfulness is being on the Way with the Way, the Truth, and the Life. Faithfulness is doing what Jesus did—connecting with and changing the very essence of the lives he touched. That is what it means to be a Christian and the church! Anything short of that is unfaithful.

So we end where we began this chapter—reaching out to enfold all of God's creation, giving sign to the world that the church truly exists for those folks who aren't *yet* a part of it.

Reflection Time

- **How much time do you personally spend on your welcoming ministries?**
- **What's keeping you from providing an additional worship service?**
- **Does your church have an intentional method of assimilating new people?**
- **Are more of your leaders serving outside the church than inside (small groups that meet in homes are considered "outside")?**

Notes

1. Bill Easum, *Unfreezing Moves* (Nashville: Abingdon, 2001).

2. For an excellent book, see Mark Waltz, *First Impressions* (Group, 2005).

3. Easum and Cornelius, *Go BIG: Lead Your Church to Explosive Growth* (Nashville: Abingdon, 2006).

4. For more see Easum and Bandy, *Growing Spiritual Redwoods* (Nashville: Abingdon, 1997), pp. 172–203.

CHAPTER TEN

Pastor, Are YOU Ready for Resurrection?

Now you know the truth. Resurrection doesn't come in a box or a program. No quick gimmicks exist. It begins with *you*. God is ready to work through you if you are ready to follow God's directions.

Don't look around to see who is willing to start the resurrection with you. Just look in the mirror and ask one question: Am I the one?

Throughout the book I have stressed that just like the resurrection of Jesus, the resurrection of your church will begin when one person decides to be the vehicle God works through. Are you the one?

If you're the one, let me recount what's in front of you.

Time in Prayer

Spend as much time in prayer as you need to discern God's will for this church. Don't trust this to a committee or vision-planning session. God doesn't work through groups. (I know, some of your friends might suggest it is naive to believe we can know God's will for a church, but they are wrong.)

Write down on paper what you learn about God's will through your prayer and journaling time. Once you discern God's will, don't let anyone change the agenda.

Deepen Your Relationship with Jesus

Decide how you are going to deepen your relationship with Jesus and how you are going to keep that relationship strong for the battle that is in front of you. Failure at this point will result in unnecessary stress along the way and most likely failure.

Talk It Over with Your Spouse

As you have already been made aware, turnaround is messy business. It will require understanding and support from home. So before beginning, make sure your spouse is on board and understands why you are opening up a hornet's nest.

Find a Mentor

Find a mentor and confidant who is doing the kind of ministry God desires to see happen in your church. Covenant to share your journey with this person and seek his or her counsel along the way. If this person has been where you are going, the relationship can save you years of mistakes. If an acceptable mentor isn't nearby, you might try reputable coaching groups such as www.valwoodcoaching.com and www.thecolumbiapartnership.com.

If there are other churches in the area attempting turnaround, you might want to cluster together with them for support and peer learning. Just don't attempt this all alone.

Help the Church See the Problem

You must help the people internalize the spiritual condition of the church. Don't pull any punches here. The more clearly they understand what has happened to their church and themselves, the more open they will be to resurrection. People change in direct proportion to their discomfort. So make them uncomfortable.

Create a Culture of Courage

Begin to create a culture of courage. Try some small victories that lead up to a major change that will rock the foundation of the church. If you spend enough time in prayer you will discover what these small victories might be.

Develop a Strategy

Strategy will vary from place to place and usually flows out of the spiritual development of the group. But it will include the basic characteristics in the previous chapter. When you're ready, have your group study my book *Unfreezing Moves*.[1] It will guide you through the process of resurrection.

Pray for Those Alienated

Pray for and serve those who are upset or alienated by the changes without asking anything in return. Not only is this your Christian responsibility, it also is one of the most disarming things you can do.

Never Blink

And remember, once you have decided on a course of action, never blink.

Time for Action

Are *you* the one?

If so, what lies in front of you can be one of the most exciting periods of your life. It's all up to *you*.

And remember one thing—God is now promising you, "I am with you always" (Matt. 28:20 NIV). So you see—you're not alone in this. You have the best partner possible. So what are you waiting for?

Reflection Time

• **Are *you* the one?**

Note

1. Bill Easum, *Unfreezing Moves* (Nashville: Abingdon, 2001).

EPILOGUE

The Meaning of Faithfulness

While writing this book, I received two pieces of mail—one snail mail and one online.

The snail mail article came from a person I'm not sure I know, but the article was from a religion professor at a prominent university. The article said that the church is called to be faithful, not necessarily effective.

The online article was sent through our advanced listserv[1] and basically said we were called to live out our faith in the ordinary things of life. The article suggested that God does not call us to be extraordinary but to be faithful in the ordinary and routine things of life.

While there is wisdom in both of the articles, there is also an insidious heresy and misunderstanding of the biblical witness. Let me explain.

Many portions of the church today have a heretical understanding of what it means to be faithful. It most certainly doesn't mean "live out your life in mundane, ordinary ways and don't worry about being effective."

Christians were not "set apart" to merely exist. In both Old and New Testaments faithfulness was tied to action. In the Old Testament it was usually to multiply and either replenish or subdue the earth. In the New Testament it was to make disciples of every people group on the earth. In both Testaments faithfulness meant achieving something out of the ordinary. That also sounds like effectiveness to me.

One of the primary heresies of our time is the way we have reduced faithfulness to the realm of the mundane and ordinary or for a church merely to hang on as if God gave his life in Christ so that we could be ordinary and mundane. I just can't buy that, not when I read the stories of Abraham and Paul and all of those in between. God has called us to a much higher plane of existence than just ordinary.

That's one of the primary problems with mainline Christianity—we're too ordinary. Our lives don't stand out or stand for much. We don't believe any longer in God doing the extraordinary through us like raising of the dead, healing of the demonic, casting out demons (controllers?), walking on water, parting the seas, or even making jackasses speak (I've met some in our churches who've learned how to be vocal)—just to mention a few. I could go on, but none of the things I could think of are ordinary.

We've so glamorized the ordinary that we have encouraged Christians and churches to be comfortable with the mundane, yea, we seek it out and bask in its glory as if ordinary and faithfulness is simply surviving. So Christians just hang on by the seat of their pants, and churches merely pray to keep the doors open, while God cries over our lack of faithfulness and effectiveness.

I doubt if the call to ordinariness is even slightly compelling to the non-Christian. It's pathetic and absurd. No non-Christian would ever be inspired by this. It's certainly not anything worth giving one's life to.

No, Christians should aspire to the extraordinary. No matter how ordinary our lives might be, God makes them extraordinary. God makes the mundane profound. God makes the weak strong. Need I go on?

When we align ourselves with God's vision, it unleashes the extraordinary and brings about the unexpected and uncontrollable. We become a "Holy people," a "chosen people," even a "royal priesthood," "blessed in order to bless others." How can anyone think it's ordinary to be a Christian? How can anyone even use the word "ordinary" when referring to a Christian? One can't, unless one wishes to water down the good news.

Epilogue: The Meaning of Faithfulness

One line in the article sent me by snail mail (I wish I had kept it, but I threw it away in disgust) suggested that it was wrong for people like me to even hint that faithful churches always grow. What a cop out! What an argument for the ordinary and ineffective church that has emerged in the Western hemisphere—mainly among mainlines. Many other groups seem to be experiencing an extraordinary, explosive expansion of the Kingdom. Could it be because they understand the biblical link between faithfulness and effectiveness? Could it be because they pray for God to unleash the Spirit on their work in a powerful way while we bask in the sun of the ordinary?

So let me set forth a biblical understanding of faithful and effectiveness. Jesus' last command to us was to "go and make disciples" of every people group. To be a faithful follower of Jesus means making disciples of all people. It's that simple. We don't need long theological debates over what faithfulness ultimately means in the New Testament. The early church writers made it very clear—they understood Jesus' last words to be "go and make disciples."

So let me make the statement again: faithful churches always grow in numbers because being a follower of Jesus means making disciples. If your whole being is tied up in making disciples, your church will grow.

Now, let me chew on that statement a moment by asking some questions.

Do you spend the majority of your time at the well talking with the Samaritan like Jesus did?

Have you trained anyone to articulate their faith to another person?

Does your church spend most of its time, energy, and money strategizing on how to reach those who aren't part of the Body of Christ?

If you or your church aren't doing the above, neither of you is faithfully following in the steps of the Master. You and church are not learning the trade Jesus died to teach you. Therefore, the odds are your church is not growing.

God has called the church to be both faithful and effective. And that ain't ordinary. That's extraordinary and effective!

God can and does make a silk purse out of a sow's ear! Christians are proof of it.

Note

1. We have an online forum that Bill Easum and Tom Bandy monitor daily where they offer collective coaching. Go to http://easumbandy.com/join.html to learn more or to join.

APPENDIX

My First Six Months as Pastor of a Church: What to Preach

Part One: The Ever-Widening Circle

No matter where you're located, no matter what size church, and no matter what situation in which you find yourself, what follows will always be a workable plan. You may have to tweak it to fit your personality, but covering these basics will always serve you well.

This series focuses on the scripture I preached during my first six months as the new pastor of the church I turned around and then was the pastor of for twenty-four years.

If I were facing my first six months as pastor of a new church, I would want to preach the following sermons to lay the foundation for my entire ministry there. I share my thoughts on these texts with the knowledge that they can be easily customized from church to church. You will see that all of the texts are chosen to get people to think outward rather than inward. Also keep in mind that you might spend several weeks exploring each of these texts.

Acts 1:8

I would begin with Acts 1:8 and what I call the *Ever-Widening Circle*.[1] I like to begin with this text for two reasons. First, it contains what the early church considered to be the last will and testament of Jesus. Nothing could be more binding than the last words of our resurrected Lord. Those who have experienced the last words of a loved one, either orally or in the form of a letter, know the importance of such words. If the last words come from a loved one, no one with any heart can ignore them.

Second, this text contains the prime directive of the church, which I call The Basic Law of Congregational Life (BLCL). This "law" is the reality that "churches grow when they intentionally reach out to others and churches die when all they do is take care of themselves." How can the Scripture be any clearer than this text? Jesus says, "Be my witness." The BLCL challenges congregations with the primary reason churches decline—self-centeredness and a feeling of entitlement. It is a reminder that life does not revolve around us or our church. Life is centered in how we treat the stranger whom God sends our way. Growing churches are more concerned about people than the preservation of the institution or making sure there is money in the bank for a rainy day.

This text eliminates any doubts about the role of the church. Just look at the graphic. It begins with each one of us, "you," and then continues to "ever-widen" out until it comes to the ends of the earth. The role of the church is to turn itself outward to the world and witness to Jesus Christ "unto the ends of the earth." Let's look closer at the text.

First, we are to be a witness to Jerusalem. I take "Jerusalem" to be the church in which we are located. The best way to nurture our church is to get the church to reach out to nurture others.

Appendix

Second, we are to be a witness to Judea, which represents the area surrounding your church. Every church must see the surrounding area as part of its parish. As Jesus wept over Jerusalem, so our churches should give of themselves to their "cities." Why not mark off a section of your community and begin to pray for its salvation?

Third, we are to be a witness to Samaria. The Samaritans were the outcasts of their day. So Jesus is telling us that we aren't the church until we reach out to the unloved and unwanted of our day. Is your church that inclusive? Or has it targeted some people as "not welcome"?

Fourth, we are to be a witness to the whole world. Churches must be involved in world missions. It doesn't matter how much a church reaches out, there is always more to be done. Churches must believe that with God's help there is no limit to their ministry—it's an ever-widening reality.

The message is clear. Our witness is to begin at home and spread out to the ends of the world. The church is not the church unless it reaches out well beyond its own four walls. Acts 1:8 lays the biblical foundation of the Great Commission.

To support this text I would include the stories of Philip in Acts 8:4-8 and Acts 8:26-40. These contain the first attempt of the early church to reach out beyond Jerusalem. Prior to Philip, the strategy of the earliest church was to hunker down and wait for the world to come to it. According to Tom Bandy, they were the "church in residence." I would be sure to discuss how difficult it is for the church to remain focused outward. Even the church at Jerusalem began to focus inward. If that could happen so soon after Christ's death, how easy it must be for churches today to turn inward.

I spent a week exploring each of the outer rings in the graphic and then took the congregation into the importance of world missions. Since my tribe (UMC) had limited world missions—mostly agricultural, medical, and disaster help—I had to emphasize that true world missions included both the spreading of the good news and the giving of a cold cup of water. Acts is full of rich texts that support world missions.

Acts 2:1-13

My second text would focus on Acts 2:1-13 and the advent of the Holy Spirit. My emphasis would be on the relationship between being a witness to Jesus Christ in Acts 1:8 and being filled with the Holy Spirit. Effective and authentic faith is explosive, uncontrollable, and spontaneous. Every time the Holy Spirit moves in Acts, people are upset, everything is turned upside down, and nothing really makes rational sense.

I'd want people to know up front that I believe faith has little to do with the rational and predictable. I'd want them to know that my ministry among them will be explosive, spiritual, and supernatural. I'd want them to know that it is God's will for them to step out on faith, even if they don't have the money. They have the money; they just don't want to lose it.

Scattered throughout Acts are numerous stories to support the theme of this sermon. Use those that tickle your fancy.

I would also give notice to the "controllers" that true spirituality is not about controlling what happens in the church. Freedom, spontaneity, and flexibility in reaching out to the nonbeliever are at the heart of the biblical church. Then I would ask, "How well does this describe the way this church functions?" You see, being new, I can play dumb and at the same time open a can of worms, if one does exist. But, I have couched my challenge in the Scripture, not in some issue that can be hotly debated.

Acts 10

My third text would be Acts 10 where Peter is forced to go eat pork with a Gentile! I know the congregation has already heard that the role of the church is to reach out to the world. But I want them to hear it again and again. Whether we like it or not, God calls every authentic leader into the world to be with people who make us uncomfortable. Like Peter, we might find when we get out into the world that God is already there. Cornelius was a God-fearer before Peter arrived.

A major part of this story is the struggle Peter experienced before he went to see Cornelius. Remember, Peter was a key leader in the Jerusalem church and clearly the leading Apostle based on Jesus' own feelings toward him. Peter was responsible for the Jerusalem church's hunkering down and focusing on internal things, like organizing the church, when he should have been on the road to mission with Jesus. It's no wonder we struggle with the need to move outside our four walls. The question before us is, Will we wrestle with the need to turn totally outward and spend more time, energy, and money on reaching the lost than we spend on ourselves? That's the question I want to haunt the congregation with during my first six months. So I would replay it over and over throughout my preaching from Acts.

Part Two: The Two Imperatives of the Early Church

In part 1 of this series, I shared the bare bones of several weeks of preaching around the theme *The Ever-Widening Circle.* I also shared what I call the "Basic Law of Congregational Life," which is that the church is most faithful when it reaches out to others with the good news.

In part 2 of this series, I want to emphasize two christological imperatives I find in the actions of the earliest Christians—*devotion* and *obedience* to Jesus who is God's anointed one (Christ).

Keep in mind that I was preaching to a basically defunct mainline church that I was asked to restart. Mainliners are notorious for not knowing what to do with Jesus or with trying to separate the Jesus of Nazareth from the Christ of faith—as if Jesus were a reality and the Christ of faith only a myth (in the best sense of the word). In my preaching I refused to make any distinction between the historical Jesus and the Christ of faith. To call Jesus "the Christ" is simply to acknowledge that Jesus is God's anointed one whom we are to call "Lord."

I'm constantly baffled by the way so many churches do mission work without any reference to Jesus Christ. What they do is no different from what a Lions Club or a Rotary Club might do. To give a cup of cold water without the name of Jesus attached to it is little more than what any good charity does. Christians have to go another step somewhere along the way. We have what no other group has to offer—the salvation of the world. To flinch from that belief is to deny the very essence of our faith. Thus the key question, "How can we be rabid for Jesus without being bigots?" I want mainliners to chew on that one for a while.

In my early years of consulting, I spent a lot of time in the Northeast. I can't tell you how many laypeople would privately say to me, "Thank you for speaking the name of Jesus. It has been a long time since we've heard his name in the pulpit." On one occasion, after four days of my consulting with a church, as the pastor dropped me off at the airport, he said, "You've mentioned a personal relationship with Jesus Christ. What do you mean by that?" If we are going to call ourselves "Christians," Jesus Christ must be a central part of our faith.

When you remove Jesus from the conversation, there is no conversation worth pursuing for the church. So the message to my nearly defunct mainline church focused on the central role Jesus plays in both our devotion and our obedience.

Acts 2:36

"Therefore let all Israel be assured of this: God has made this Jesus, whom you crucified, both Lord and Christ."

Based on scripture, I wanted to nail down two clear models that are also imperatives for the local church: the earliest churches' devotion to Jesus Christ and the earliest churches' obedience to Jesus. The early church was clearly christological, both in its obedience and its devotion. Its message was about God as experienced in Jesus. It refused to make any separation between "Jesus" and "Christ."

To sit on God's throne and to be called Lord and Christ is to separate Jesus from all other humans and to equate him with God. As such, he commands our devotion and obedience.

Devotion to Jesus

In the early stages of Christianity, devotion to God and to Jesus was common. Throughout Acts, the term "Lord" is used twice as many times for Jesus as for God. The explicit devotion to Jesus (not the Christ) is unparalleled in Jewish literature. Jesus was worshiped in prayers where people prayed directly to him (Acts 7:59), in invocations to intervene in life's affairs that one could only attribute to a god (1 Cor. 5), and in baptisms (Acts 8:16, 10:48). In the Lord's Supper (1 Cor. 11:20), Jesus played a role that hitherto had been reserved only for the gods. In addition, Jesus was worshiped directly through hymns (Eph. 5:19) and in prophecy (2 Cor. 12:9).

But let's be clear: Jesus was worshiped only because God asked Christians to do so (John 5:23).

Jesus was revered and prayed to so often that, over time, the church felt it necessary to convene a council to determine what the relationship of Jesus was to God. After all, monotheism is at the heart of Judaism and Christianity. You know the final verdict—Jesus was very God and very human. Needless to say, Jesus is at the center of any form of authentic Christianity.

Obedience to Jesus

Obedience to Jesus is a natural result of such devotion. Obedience to God can be found only through Jesus. But what does this obedience look like? Sitting in a pew? Going to committees? We all know Christ didn't die for such nonsense.

Obedience to Jesus is just another way of saying that the earliest church saw its reason for existence to be missional. To be obedient to Jesus was to do what Jesus did—relate to the nonbeliever and challenge the professional Christian. To be obedient to Jesus was to be with him on the road to mission, to be moving away from Jerusalem toward Emmaus (a Roman garrison filled with Gentiles).

Therefore, all theology and all ministry are defined by missions. Every Christian must be a minister of Jesus Christ. All people who call themselves Christians should consider themselves to be missionaries!

The focus of authentic ministry is outward rather than inward. The pinnacle of Christian maturity is when our primary concern is the salvation of the world rather than the entitlements that come with church membership. It was in this context that I told my mainline congregation I would spend 80 percent of my time helping them win San Antonio to Christ instead of visiting them in their homes or in the hospital.

Throughout my message to them about devotion and obedience, I continually weaved these two points: the mission of the church is to share Jesus with the world; to remove Jesus from the conversation is to cease being the church.

Part Three: Creating a Solid Community of Faith

Immediately after Jesus said that God's mission is like an ever-widening circle, reaching out to more and more people, the Holy Spirit was poured forth into the world so that Peter's sermon resulted in thousands of people being welcomed into the Body of Christ (Acts 1 and 2).

At the very outset of the story of the church, the multiplication of disciples is showcased for all to see (even though most of them still didn't get it). Clearly, God is saying that the purpose of the church is to win the world to faith in God through Jesus Christ. All through Acts the story is clear—God wants the church to have explosive growth.

Part three of my plan takes a bit of a departure from the constant outreach theme of the first few weeks of preaching. The focus of this message is on the coexisting need to reach inward and establish the core values of the church. Keep in mind that by this time I have spent several weeks on the need of the church to reach out. I will also quickly return to the theme of outreach after one or two messages on establishing the DNA of the mission.

Before a church can experience explosive growth, it must reach in and prepare itself to receive such growth. However, I would never begin my preaching at a new church by focusing the church inward. I always want the focus of the believer to be on the nonbeliever, even when attention is being given to developing the inner life of the congregation.

But the church must get its act together inwardly so it can be a witness to the nonbeliever. Thus, the heart of this message is that Christians must grow and be united so that the church can be an incubator of faith for those who have not yet heard. For this to take place the church must have a clear DNA; must be united in its mission and hold one another accountable to that mission; and must not allow the needs of the church to hold it back from reaching out to the world.

Acts 2:42-47

One of the most powerful aspects of the early church was the clarity and solidarity with which it moved forward. They literally had "all things in common." In our language today, we call this "DNA." They were clear about their mission, vision, core values, and bedrock beliefs.

However, this clarity did not come out of a vacuum. It arose out of their common devotion and obedience to God as seen through Jesus Christ. For authentic DNA to be discovered, those doing the discovering must be devoted and obedient to Jesus Christ. Otherwise, the process is flawed from the beginning. Any authentic devotion and obedience to Jesus Christ always results in a passion for those who have not yet heard and experienced what Jesus has to offer. People who don't care about discipleship haven't experienced the fullness of redemption yet.

Whatever method you use to develop and embed DNA, you must never allow people to forget that the primary reason they are doing this is to foster a church environment so rich and unified that it becomes an incubator of faith for the nonbeliever. We want nonbelievers to sense God's love for them just by being around Christians. Peter Scholtes's song hits the bull's-eye: "They will know we are Christians by our love."

What most of us overlook in this section of Acts is Peter's call to repentance. Peter knew that God's people needed to repent of their feelings of superiority and entitlement. First-century Judaism was much like mainstream Christianity today. It felt entitled to God's good pleasure and had little concern for the non-Hebrew. It felt it was chosen because it was special rather than feeling that it was special because it was chosen.

Christians must never feel entitled to God or their pastors, nor can they afford to be unconcerned for the non-Christian. Therefore, many of our churches need to repent of their feelings of entitlement and unconcern before they can begin to work on their DNA. I wanted my people to get "right" with God and their neighbor before beginning to work on their DNA. Our people need to repent from their selfishness, and we need to tell them that.

Appendix

I wanted to hit the entitlement issue head-on. I wish I had hit it much harder than I did because nothing ruins a church more than multiple strands of DNA. It would take me years to figure that one out.

So I cast a vision of a new DNA—a church where "everyone is a minister of Jesus Christ." If I were to do that today, it would be "Everyone is a missionary of Jesus Christ." Of course, most people shouldn't cast a new vision during their first few weeks or months as pastor of a new church, unless it is a new church plant or a restart. Most will want to call the church to this task as Tom Bandy suggests in *Moving Off the Map*. Or some might want to gather the key spiritual leaders and hammer out a consensus as I describe in *Unfreezing Moves*. Do whatever comes natural to you, but rally the church around a single mission because God wants the church to be united around a common mission.

Acts 4–5

God also wants the church to be united in its community and its message. So I told the congregation the story of Ananias and Sapphira. This story wasn't just thrown in by the author. It sets forth two fundamental issues: accountability and the importance of unity.

Because the early church had such a close community, any deviation from that unity was seen as a major threat to the mission. Any sign of deviation from the perceived truth was attacked with a vengeance. Christians should hold one another accountable when they break the unity of the church. Healthy churches do not tolerate any form of disunity.

Think how it would change your church if all members were held accountable for the vows they took when becoming members? Can you imagine the grief that might be eliminated today if in the past the light of the gospel had been shined on conflicted people? They might have been changed.

How Much More of an Incubator of Faith Could Your Church Become If You Held Every Leader Accountable? Acts 6:1-7

There is a lot of difference between taking care of people and transforming them. You can take care of them without transforming them, but you can't transform them without taking care of them. The twelve were right—it is never the duty of the leaders to care for one another, but to see to it that everyone is cared for. Why? So that the church will be so loving that it is an incubator for those who have not experienced Jesus.

At this point, even though I don't like talking about "lay" ministry, I would use this passage as the justification for lay ministries.

I agree with Tom Bandy. The earliest church came really close to turning inward. But, thank God, as time and events unfolded, they did not.

As you prepare to preach any message, keep in mind that the most outward-facing church is just one decision away from turning inward! So gather the DNA, but don't let the church become comfortable focusing on itself.

Part Four: Fast Growth Is Biblical and God Expects It Today

We must now get back to the major theme of my first six months: God wants the church to reach out to the unchurched.

Acts 1 and 2 tell us that the early church went from 120 believers to 3,120 believers overnight.

But that's not all. Acts 2:47 tells us that, "And the Lord added to their number daily those who were being saved." The number of Christians was growing daily! Acts 4:4 says that many of the people who heard their message believed it so that the number of believers totaled about four thousand men, not counting women and children. So, how many people are we actually talking about here?

Conservative estimates at this point put the number of believers around 20,000. In the first year after Christ's death, the number of believers went from 120 to 20,000. Not only is Crazy-Go-Big-Huge-Growth possible, it's biblical and God wants it!

That's the blueprint God gave us. (Keep in mind that this was a bankrupt church ready to close and, because of my first few weeks, was actually dwindling in size.)

What's keeping you from asking God to multiply your ministry? Right now, would you just ask God to explode the dream you have? Would you ask God to help you reach the entire city?

What do you think God is going to say? "No, I don't want to do that"? Of course God wants to multiply ministry. So what's holding God back if we know it's biblical; if we know it's the blueprint that God gives us? We are! That's who. Now what are we going to do about it?

God is just getting warmed up. Acts 5:28 says, "You have filled Jerusalem with your teaching [about Jesus]." Acts 6:7 says, "The number of disciples in Jerusalem increased rapidly." It is only now that they use the word "rapidly." When going from zero to 20,000, Luke didn't use the word "rapidly." But then, it's as if he's saying, now that the believers are warmed up, they're *really* going to start growing their numbers. This is crazy, spectacular growth. It just takes off like a wildfire. And that's what God wants to do in our ministries.

This wildfire of growth was consistent and compelling. Acts 21 uses another word to describe the growth—"myriads." That means tens of thousands of believers are now in Jerusalem. The number of believers at this point in the story is staggering. Especially when you realize that Jerusalem had only around 55,000 inhabitants at the time.

You see, God wants us to win our city to Christ. We're not just going to build a church; we're going to change a city. At this point, the people of my church began to gather into two camps—those who thought I was crazy and those whose eyes began to light up. As the weeks went by, it became easier and easier to tell the difference between those who got it and those who would never get it.

What are you doing in your preaching that is causing people to wonder about your sanity? Are you willing to ask them to join you in the quest to transform your city? Or are you hung up on the numbers? If so, you will never grow a faithful, biblical church. Growth is biblical.

How can such staggering growth begin? Where do we start? Such growth is dependent on deep commitment, reaching out to the unchurched, and personal conversion.

Acts 7

Stephen is the first Christian martyr on record. He took his commitment seriously, and it cost him all that he had. He wasn't "playing" church. Stephen was stoned to death, and then Saul began his rampage against the church. This was not a good time to be committed to Christ, but that is what such growth demands—commitment.

At this point, I challenged my congregation to step up to another level of commitment and take the four vows of our denomination seriously: "I will support my church with my prayers, presence, gifts, and service." I shared with them that everyone who joined from now on and anyone in leadership would be held accountable to those vows.

Acts 8

Philip is the first person on record to reach out to the least, last, and lost. He connected with the people most hated by the Jews—Samaritans. Philip led the Ethiopian to Christ and then went wandering through the countryside proclaiming Jesus. His excitement was off the chart.

But that's the way it is with all Christians when they lead someone to Christ. When was the last time you led someone to Christ? You don't know what you're missing. I challenged each of them to begin making relationships with someone who doesn't believe and in time to bring them to church.

What prejudices are getting in the way of you talking with your neighbor about Jesus? What fears are holding you back?

Acts 9

Most of us know the Apostle Paul. He wrote much of the New Testament. But how well do we know Paul when he was Saul? Saul was responsible for the imprisonment and death of countless Christians. His rage against them was legendary.

Then Saul met Jesus and nothing was the same, not even his name.

Before we can experience the kind of growth God has in store for us, we need to get "right" with God. Some of us need to repent of our selfish, ingrown ways. Some of us need the salvation that only Christ can offer.

At this point I became very clear with my congregation. The actions of some of the people prior to and after my arrival were downright heathen, and I could not tell from their actions whether or not they were even Christians. I singled out some of the behavior I had experienced during those first few months and called for those who were feeling that way to repent or leave. It was dead silent that morning. Over the next few weeks more people left than repented or gave their lives to Christ. But the transition was underway. The exodus would not be complete for four or five more months.

(At this point we are somewhere between three and four months into the turnaround as a new pastor.)

Part Five: The Church Exists for
Those Who Aren't Yet Present

I really didn't like Doug. He was rough, his language was foul, and sometimes he smelled. But he played a good game of golf, and golfers of my caliber were hard to find in seminary. So I *sort of* befriended him.

One day he asked me why I went to seminary. He actually opened the door for me, but I didn't want to walk through it and share my story. We had been playing golf together for a couple of months. That was our only relationship. Other than that I didn't even like him. But for some reason he not only liked me, but he trusted me. So my conscience got the best of me, and later in the nineteenth hole I shared Christ with him. And guess what, he was ready to hear and accepted Christ. I felt elated, but also ashamed.

Ever had such an experience?

Surely you have. If so, begin this message with your story and tell them how you felt. Let them see your squirming, as well as your joy in the end. If you have never led a person to Christ, you shouldn't preach this message. Instead, I encourage you to ask God to send someone your way with whom you can share your faith, and then describe to the congregation how this was a first for you and how you felt doing it and then invite them to do the same.

You see, most people never share their faith with anyone. And most don't feel badly about not doing so. But some will have their conscience pricked and will seek to share their faith. As they see you struggle they will gain the courage to do the same.

Acts 10

The story of Peter and Cornelius is a priceless look into how people react to sharing their faith and the role God plays in evangelism. It is a great picture of the reluctance of people to engage in sharing their faith, and the surprise they have when most of the work of redemption is already done before they open their mouth. Spend at least one message on this text. If you have a lot of experiences to share, develop it into two or three messages.

We Are Called to Do Things That May Feel Uncomfortable

Up until this time, no one had been baptized into the Christian faith other than Jews or Samaritans. For Gentiles to enter the faith was unheard of. Cornelius was a Gentile.

The fact that Peter didn't want to go to Cornelius is so powerful when people understand the dynamics. God was asking Peter to do something so distasteful to a Jew that it would make most Jews throw up. "You want me to do *what*, God? Surely you're not asking me to eat pork with a Gentile? My God, Jews don't do that. Jews don't eat pork and certainly not with Gentiles."

Life is full of things none of us likes to do, but that are beneficial to our personal growth in the long run. Because God knows our hearts, God often asks us to do the very thing that challenges us the most. God looks into our hearts and asks us to do the very thing we don't want to do because God knows that in doing so we grow. Show them how Jesus responded differently to people based on what he felt they needed. (The rich young ruler was one example. You can find several more examples based on what you know about your church.)

Few of us enjoy exercise, but without it we grow old prematurely. And what about saving for the future when you badly want to spend the money on something today? I can't remember all of the examples I used, but you get the point. I'm sure you have some things in your life that you didn't enjoy doing but paid great dividends over the long haul. Share those with them.

Can't you just hear your people saying, "Pastor, surely you're not asking me to talk to my neighbor about Jesus. Get real." But that is exactly what you want to ask them to do over the next six months. Tell them you will do it with them. Let them know you have the same fears they do, and if you've overcome the fear of sharing your faith, tell them how you did it. If not, share your journey with them over the next few months. When people actually share their faith, let some of them give their testimony during worship. It will encourage others to do the same.

I doubt if most of the people in your congregation want to become involved enough with their neighbor that they can invite them to church, much less to their small group—or even more, to share their faith with them. Every study shows that sharing one's faith is one of the hardest aspects of being a Christian. I forget the exact statistics, but it takes about 75 people to share faith with one person.

Find your own ways to milk this section, because most of your people are either afraid to share their faith or have some form of arrogance toward those around them.

Fear Is Not Unusual

Here I shared with them the first time I shared my faith with someone. I related to them how nervous I was. I recounted the many times I visited newcomers to the church and prayed as I knocked on the door, "Lord, don't let them be home!" All of us are afraid to witness at times. It's natural—we're invading people's most private moments. We're an intruder of the worst kind. But God expects it of some of us.

Sharing Faith Is the Essence of the Church

Even though I was also quick to point out that not everyone is called or gifted to share their faith, I still had to drive home the fact that every church is expected to share Jesus Christ with the world. That is what the church exists to do. No exceptions exist. Churches don't have the luxury of putting themselves at the center of their ministry. But everyone is expected to support the effort by their church to reach out and share Jesus Christ. What I wanted to do at this point was to show them that sharing faith is the essence of the church. Not programs or quilting or whatever, but sharing Jesus.

We Can Resist and Be Unfulfilled or We Can Respond and Find Peace

The nightmare God kept sending to Peter finally wore him down. Finally, Peter gave up and went to Cornelius. Well, I want you to know—God isn't going to give up, so you might as well go on and do it. God bugged Peter over and over, and God won't let you rest either. You might as well give up also and begin developing relationships with non-Christians or unchurched people.

Cornelius Was Ready

I finished with "Don't be afraid; God will go before you." When Peter got to Cornelius, he found that God was already at work. Cornelius was reading scripture. All Peter had to do was confirm what Cornelius was experiencing. Often that is the case after you spend time with your neighbor. They have seen the Christ within you, and it has rubbed off on them.

I'm not talking about cold turkey evangelism. I'm talking about making friends, establishing a relationship, waiting until they are ready, and if they are never ready, then at least you have a new friend.

But if you spend time nurturing a relationship with your neighbor, it is not unlikely that your faith will begin to prepare their hearts even if you haven't said a word about your faith.

Often this is the case with relational evangelism. If we have gotten to know the person well and become part of their lives, we begin to feel the rhythm of their lives. We develop a sixth sense as to when to share our faith. Often the friend opens the door the same way Cornelius did with Peter or Doug did with me that day on the nineteenth hole.

Conclusion

We couldn't close without referring to the fact that Cornelius had gathered his friends together to hear what Peter had to say. He wanted others to be blessed by Peter's ministry. And we should do the same. If our hearts overflow with God's love in Christ, it is only natural that we want to share it with others.

Part Six: The Door Is Flung Open

I'll never forget the first time I heard the good news. I was sixteen and it blew me away. Six months later, I was on the third hole of Hancock Golf Course when I finally said yes to Christ. By my seventeenth birthday I was preaching somewhere almost every week—missions, street corners, and even a few churches. Those were such wonderful times of discovery for me.

How about you? When did Christ first come into your life? Can you remember that awesome moment when you realized that God loved you in spite of yourself? Is that moment as real to you now as it was back then?

I want us to focus today on the need of this church to have as its primary mission reaching everyone in this community for Christ to the point that each person is a minister of Jesus Christ (today I would use "missionary" instead of "minister").

So far in this series we have witnessed the movement of God recorded in the first ten chapters of the Acts of the Apostles. We have heard the last will and testament of Jesus; seen the coming of the Holy Spirit; talked about the two imperatives of the gospel; witnessed what can happen when a church turns inward and when members become conflicted; and were with Phillip and Peter in their brief encounters with Gentile, non-Jewish converts.

Now we come to one of the most remarkable events in the New Testament—the shift from targeting Israel with the good news to the inclusion of the Gentile. You have to realize that at this point in history a Jew and Gentile were lifelong enemies. It was considered unclean for a Jew to associate with a Gentile.

So up until this point in the history of Christianity there had been only two isolated accounts of the good news being shared with Gentiles—Phillip's baptism of the Samaritan eunuch and Peter's conversation with Cornelius. But now we come to the event that flung open the door for Christianity to go to the entire world.

After the stoning of Stephen, many of the converts fled to other countries, and even though most of those converts spoke only to Jews, *some* shared the good news with the Gentiles in Antioch. Now, so we're all clear, the word "Gentile" meant anyone who wasn't Jewish. That means the door was flung open for you and me. Give that some thought. To this point in our story, the good news was mainly for the Jewish race.

But watch!

Acts 11:18-21: The Church Exists for Those Who Aren't Yet with Us

As a result of the ministry of the unnamed disciples, "a great number of people believed and turned to the Lord" (Acts 11:21). "God has granted even the Gentiles repentance unto life" (Acts 11:18). "No! We believe it is through the grace of our Lord Jesus that we are saved, just as they [Gentiles] are" (Acts 15:11).

What a wonderful event. Now you and I are included in God's mission. And as a result the church in Antioch grew and grew.

I can just hear some people today saying, "See there, the only way the church can grow is by watering down the gospel." Well, they are not alone.

You would think that the explosion of growth in Antioch would please the mother church in Jerusalem, wouldn't you? But not so. Instead, they sent Barnabas down to sniff out what was going on. And guess what? Barnabas is captured by the movement of God and not only begins to minister to the Gentiles but enlists the services of Paul, and the church in Antioch explodes even more.

Time to Talk Turkey

We have a problem in our church. Some of your present leaders are acting much like those in Jerusalem. They don't really want the church to grow, at least not by conversion growth. They want it to remain a close-knit social club of do-gooders. I want everyone to hear this—that kind of attitude stops today. It simply isn't welcome here anymore. The church exists not for us but for those who aren't yet part of our church.

So listen carefully: everyone is welcome here who welcomes everyone else. If you don't welcome everyone else you aren't welcome here anymore from this day forward (this phrase stuck with the good people and became the seedbed for our value of inclusion). You will have to take your bigotry somewhere else. Needless to say, some were not happy at this point in the message. (Keep in mind that at this point in the turnaround we still didn't have many visitors in worship. I would not preach this way if the church had lots of visitors. I would do it in board meetings.)

You may not have such a problem in your church, but I bet many of you have church leaders who don't go out of their way to reach out to the unchurched around them. If so, this is where you can use the story of the Jerusalem Conference to speak to them.

Appendix

Acts 15:5-11: Even the Early Church Had Trouble Reaching Out

From Antioch, Paul and others spread the good news across the region. Thousands of Gentiles heard and responded. The movement of God spread over the land.

The same thing happens today when people give themselves to the mission of Christ and reach out to those in need of good news. More people are won to Christ when we leave the church than when we hide behind its four walls. It's time that we developed a serious plan for reaching San Antonio with the good news.

However, the more the good news spread and the more the movement relied on the Holy Spirit rather than rituals, the more the mother church got nervous. What bothered them was that Paul wasn't taking people through the Jewish rite of circumcision before salvation. They were hanging on to the old baggage of Judaism. It would be much like us saying if you're not a baptized member of our church you aren't a Christian. That totally negates the grace of God. You and I are saved by grace and nothing more. Salvation is a gift that we can't earn or ever deserve—certainly not something we can attain through some dumb ritual.

Christians Always Welcome the Nonbeliever

So they had a powwow, much like the church conference we're going to have in a couple of months where we will decide if we are really ready to bite the bullet and pull out all of the stops to make this a great church with thousands of people. This powwow was called the Jerusalem Conference. It was there that Peter showed his true colors and finally said salvation is by grace alone. All the mother church asked from the Gentiles was that they abstain from certain items from pagan worship.

And why did Peter take this stand? Because God had prepared him for it when God forced Peter to go to Cornelius, and there he saw, for the first time, God working a miracle in the life of a non-Jew. Peter was so sold-out to the mission of God that he wouldn't let anything stand in the way of another person experiencing this wonder, no matter what the race or culture.

Even the hunkered-down Jerusalem church melted when it heard how many Gentiles were coming to Christ as a result of Paul breaking one of their most sacred of all rules. And I expect the same kind of Christian response from our board when people complain about the changes we've made in worship.

My friends, if a Jew can drop his most sacred ritual for the cause of Christ, you and I ought to be able to change worship styles to reach out to people we don't know. It's time for you to quit the bickering about the changes we've made in worship and act like mature Christians who will do anything to advance the cause of Christ.

Now, if you think the changes we've made are radical, wait till you see the next service we're going to start when this service fills up. (We're still in one service with around 60 people.)

Friends, let's be honest. The issue at the Jerusalem Conference wasn't the Jewish rite, but rather can we really believe that our lifelong enemies are also the object of God's love? But that's the whole point of the good news—that everyone, even people you don't like, are equal recipients of God's love and that the role of any Christian is to invite them to feast on that love. Aren't you glad that's true? You and I wouldn't be here today otherwise.

We stand today in the same place as Peter. God is asking us to relieve ourselves of some of our baggage—our rituals, our prejudices, our personal preferences in worship, our (you fill in the blank). What will your response be? Will you allow the mission of Christ to be so real in your life that you have to say with Peter, "God makes no distinction between us and them" or "I'll be happy with any form of worship, any program, if it brings more people to Christ"? How could your response be anything else if you love Jesus? It can't! It just simply can't.

Conclusion

So, I put the question before you—will we open our doors to people we don't know, understand, or even like? Will we have the same missionary spirit as those who were scattered abroad after the stoning of Stephen? Or will you continue to hunker down in the bunker of this nice, cozy social club? The choice is yours; but as for me, I'm going to go out each day and night of every week to be with the modern-day Gentile until this room is so full it is uncomfortable.

A small group and I that have been meeting on Friday nights are going door-to-door every Saturday asking people one question: "What it is that you need that you aren't getting from the churches in your area?" I'm inviting you to join me this Saturday to walk the neighborhood for Christ, and in the example of Philip, Peter, Paul, and Barnabas, continue to spread the good news to everyone in our area. Will you join us this Saturday as we fling open the door for everyone in San Antonio?

Part Seven: Strong Churches

By this point I am at the close of my first six months as pastor. I have trained a small cadre of leaders and we have canvassed about 2,000 homes to see what they need from the church. A board meeting is scheduled for this Sunday evening. We have a proposal before the board that will change the course of the church and begin it on its slow climb to become the second-largest church in our conference (the proposal is to borrow enough money to begin a preschool and to change the style of worship). What I would learn that night is that one-half of the present 40 attendees will leave as a result of this evening. It's showtime.

And now the essence of the message that Sunday morning.

Our reading of the life of the early church should have taught us one thing about how strong churches should function. If we want to be an authentic church of Jesus Christ, we must be willing to give ourselves on behalf of our God, our neighbors, and one another. Every example from Acts so far has shown us that authentic Christianity is lived on behalf of others, not self. Every example has shown us that God's church can change the course of history.

This means that everything we do as a people should be to honor God, reach out in love to our neighbor, and support one another. No church can achieve such stature before God by caring for itself more than it cares for those who are not yet with us.

Therefore, the primary thrust of our church must be outward and not inward. We must evaluate every issue by how it will honor God, transform our neighbor, and unite us in love. We must never make the mistake most of the congregations of our denomination have made: we must never make the survival of our church the main issue.

I know these may sound like silly words for a congregation still facing bankruptcy. I'm still not getting paid. But mark it well— God honors those who honor God. What you have been doing the past few years has not honored God; it has honored a socialist way of life that puts the well-being of society before the advancement of God's kingdom. You should know by now that I am changing that. From now on you must cease worrying about survival and go on the offence for the Kingdom. It is time we became a church and closed the social club.

Acts 15:36–18:31:
God's Mission Is to Make Churches Strong

"He went through Syria and Cilicia, strengthening the churches. . . . So the churches were strengthened in the faith and grew daily in numbers" (Acts 15:41, 16:5).

The rest of Acts consists of Paul's missionary journeys. Paul revisits all of the churches he had been in previously with one purpose in mind—to make them stronger.

That is my calling for this church—that we are strong enough to do what the early churches did: change the course of their society. We're not just building a church; we're building a people that will change the city. We're not concerned about members; we're concerned about making disciples who will turn this city upside down. We're not concerned about our survival anymore. Now we are concerned about being an instrument of God for the good of those around us. We shouldn't be concerned about the naysayers; we should be listening to the voice of God. We shouldn't worry about the cost, because Jesus didn't worry about the cost of our redemption.

I'm asking you to join me tonight in casting your vote for the advancement of the Kingdom, not the survival of the church. God wants this church to be strong and vibrant. God wants this church to change the city. And I'm asking you to join me in that quest.

Now I want you to notice a few things about strong churches.

Strong Churches Challenge the Evils of Society

I referenced Acts 16:16-40. You might choose another text to show this point and then talk about any events in the life of your church in the past where this might have happened.

For those of you concerned about the social ills of society, I promise you the day will come when this church will exercise an immense influence on the actions of this city. But for now we will put this part of our ministry on hold until we are strong enough to make a difference. (There were a number of people who felt strongly about social justice; unfortunately, they were the first to leave when we focused on Jesus. That was a shame, since social justice became one of our strongest ministries the last half of my twenty-four-year ministry among them.) (You should keep in mind that unless you are an African-American church, Hispanic church, or downtown church you should avoid social issues until you are strong.)

Strong Churches Use the Culture in Order to Reach the Culture

I referenced Paul at Mars Hill (Acts 17). I took some time here because it was the foundation for changing the worship style. We must not be afraid of using parts of the culture to reach culture. Nowhere is this truer than in the way we worship. Our worship must change. It must reflect the culture so that people are comfortable. In no way will the gospel be watered down or changed. It will remain the same, but our worship style must change so that the unchurched feel comfortable enough to hear the dangerous gospel. If the vote is passed tonight, next Sunday will be totally different. And I remind you that no form of worship is presented in the scriptures as the most authentic. Just think of the style of worship as the package in which the gospel is presented. Don't confuse the style with the essence. Worship must be done in a way that people can experience God through it. That can't happen if worship is foreign to them.

Strong Churches Grow and Make No Excuse for Their Growth

I'm tired of those of you who say that you want the church to remain small. I'm tired of those of you who say you don't think we should be concerned with numbers. I'm tired of those who say all I'm concerned about is building my own little kingdom. I'm tired of my colleagues who say that I want to water down the gospel in order to grow. The Bible is clear—strong churches add to their numbers daily. If you don't believe that and aren't willing to pray for that, then you should find another church. It's just that simple, because this church is going to grow!

Strong Churches Know That Being on the Road to Mission with Jesus Is the Primary Ministry of the Church

I made reference to the fact that most of the rest of Acts is about Paul's missionary journeys.

If we are to be faithful to the gospel, most of our ministry must have an outward thrust to it. We must gauge our success by how many adult baptisms we have; by how many recommitments of faith we see; by how many ministers of Jesus Christ we produce. (I still feel badly that I didn't see the whole picture then or I would have said, "by how many missionaries of Jesus Christ we produce.") This means that our mission is not how many members we have or how big we become. Our mission is about growing a people who will transform a city. That's our goal. And I think it is one worth sacrificing for.

Strong Churches Are Prepared to Suffer for the Gospel

Several times during the last few years of Paul's life he was persecuted and even thrown into jail. The one experience that I can't get away from is when Paul and Silas are thrown into jail in Philippi (Acts 16). While awaiting their sentence, three things happened: they sang praises to God; the doors of the jail burst open; and the jailer asked, "What must I do to be saved?" Suffering isn't always what it seems to be. Sometimes it is the prelude to God's future.

My friends, what we will propose tonight is worth suffering for. And believe me, if you adopt the proposal it will cause you some suffering. For some the suffering will be the loss of some friendships; for others it will be the loss of some church traditions that are dear to you. But for all who choose to go forward with this proposal the suffering will be financial. We will all have to decide how much the mission is worth.

It's time to show what we're made of. It's time to quit hunkering down and begin reaching out to all of San Antonio. It's time to be a church once again.

End of Series

That night 40 people showed up. The vote was 21-19 in favor of a new direction. Over the next few months most of the 19 left. I felt bad about that then; today I don't. I now know they were the primary problem.

Please be sure that whatever you do you do it in love. Don't copy what I did. I had nothing to lose. Do what you are comfortable doing. But remember, there is more to life than changing spiritual diapers.

Note

1. I've written about the "ever-widening circle" in *The Church Growth Handbook* and *The Complete Ministry Audit*.

253
E139SE LINCOLN CHRISTIAN COLLEGE AND SEMINARY

116790

3 4711 00179 0627